70 YEARS AT RINGSIDE: A HISTORY OF WRESTLING IN NEW ZEALAND

70 YEARS AT RINGSIDE: A HISTORY OF WRESTLING IN NEW ZEALAND

by
DAVE CAMERON

Copyright © Dave Caveron 2014

The right of Dave Cameron to be identified as the author of the work has been asserted by him in accordance with the Copyright, Designs and Patents act 1988.

Published by Tora Book Publishing
ISBN 978-0-9543924-7-5

All rights reserved. No part of this publication may be reproduced, stored in a retrieval system, or transmitted in any form or by any means, without prior written permission of the publisher, nor be otherwise circulated in any form of cover or binding other than that in which it is published and without a similar condition being imposed on the subsequent purchaser.

All of the photographs and scans (programmes etc.) are from the personal collection of David Cameron, but no copyright ownership is inferred. The author has made every reasonable effort to trace the copyright owners for any or all of the photographs in this book, but there may be some omissions of credits, for which I apologize. Any amendments, additions or corrections can be forwarded to the publisher.

Cover Design by Harry Otty © 2014

Dedication

This book is dedicated to my Mum and Dad for giving me half a crown 2/6, to attend my first wrestling and boxing match at the Hastings Municipal Theatre in 1946. This was my birthday present.

I would also dedicate the book to my wife Shirley, who has had to put up with wrestling and boxing books scattered around the lounge floor every night for over fifty years. I call it my homework, but she has other names for it.

Also to my son, Paul, his wife Debbie and their beautiful daughters - my granddaughters - Greer and Isla.

Contents

Introduction   i-iv

George Hackenschmidt and the early years   1

Ike Robin and Stanislaus Zbyszko   9

The 1930s   20

The 1940s   79

Eric "The Chest" Holmback   115

The Lofty Blomfield Story   121

Paul Boesch   145

The Forgotten Kiwis   148

New Zealand wrestler visits his homeland   156

"Blind Peter" and Gordon Hutter   161

Introduction

In 1945 I started cutting out maps of the second world war and putting the pictures in a scrapbook. About that time a picture of champion boxer Joe Louis came in the paper and then a picture of Lofty Blomfield, the New Zealand champion wrestler. That was how it all started. Today I am still making scrapbooks.

I first took an interest in boxing and wrestling from the radio days in 1946. My parents let me go to a boxing and a wrestling contest for my 13th birthday in 1946. After the war my favourite sports were back in full swing on radio, and were broadcast most nights of the week except Sundays. Then I would tune in to the Australian stations and it would be 12-45 before I would get to sleep. My mother was always checking to see if the radio was still going and I would be under the sheets with my torch making notes, always managing to get the radio off before getting caught. I should add that we lived in old Kauri built Church Manse's and the sound carried when one walked down the long passageways, hence I always knew when my Mum was coming to check on me.

I loved writing letters and I used to get more mail than my Dad, who was a Presbyterian Minister, as I was in all the top American wrestlers fan clubs. Right through the 1950's fan clubs for wrestlers were huge. For a few dollars you would get a badge and a membership card and monthly bulletins on your favorites progress. I remember being in Pat O'Connor's fan club for many years. The club president would present Pat with lovely ring jackets made of silk material as they were the in thing in those days. Wrestlers looked the part with lovely jackets or long robes.

I only wagged school once and that was in 1949. None of my family ever found out. Pat O'Connor was a top amateur wrestler, and my pen friend around 1947 and 1948. Pat said to me in his letter that the New Zealand Amateur wrestling Championships were coming to my hometown of Gisborne, and make sure to pop in and say hello to me. I took this to heart and on the Friday I went to school as normal on the school bus. Getting off the bus I headed straight to the Gisborne Opera House where the national championships were held over three days. I spent most of the day there, met my idol Pat O'Connor and headed back to get on the school bus at 3-15. My school teacher hounded me for a note for some days and I eventually persuaded my neighbour Mrs Wilson to write a note saying I had been sick on the Friday and unable to attend school. Of course I cycled five miles to the Gisborne Opera house on the Saturday and spent the whole day there before cycling home. I got to spend time with my hero Pat O'Connor on the Saturday also.

I starting doing notes for the American Ring magazine in 1949 and then started doing bits for overseas wrestling and other boxing publications. I remember getting a story in an English wrestling magazine called "Mat" about that time also. I had material in a French magazine and I paid a guy to translate my English into French, several Japanese magazines, and many American publications like Wrestling Revue and Ring Wrestling, and the Canadian magazines. The Japanese magazines were great and I loved doing stories in them. They were all translated into Japanese by my friend Wally Yamaguchi, who came to visit me on several occasions over the years. Wally was a wrestler himself and used to practice moves on our front lawn with our son Paul and various neighbours children.

In New Zealand I did some work for All Sports Monthly, later to become Sports Digest, and work in the Auckland Saturday sports paper the 8 O'clock. I put out wrestling programmes for Ernie Pinches from the South Pacific Wrestling Association in the mid-1960's. I used the alias of "Cauliflower" and "Canvasback" and it was a long time before anyone found out it was me. I recall John DaSilva's wife Beryl saying it was someone pretty knowledgeable about the sport of wrestling, as the facts were spot on.

I lived in England for seven years and continued to do bits in magazines around Europe. I also did work for Bert Sugar at Ring Magazine in the 1980s, and was on the Ring Ratings Panel for some years. I loved getting the free books Bert put out, and that was payment for helping him. I received the last two Ring Record books ever put out in this way. Sadly one of them was borrowed and never returned, and it had a very nice autographed piece from Bert inside.

In recent years I have mostly contributed to the NZ Martial Arts magazine, Fight Times, as I still love writing about the old time boxers and wrestlers, and Tank and Trish Todd at Fight Times are great people.

I still love doing bits about New Zealand boxing history in the boxing programmes, and I love getting a story in Duco Events programme booklets. I worked on a boxing book with Paul Lewis for a couple of years and it came out in 2012. It was called "The New Zealand Boxing Scrapbook".

It was always my ambition to write a wrestling book about New Zealand history, and when historian and boxing coach Harry Otty from Liverpool in England offered to help me I was delighted such a book could be printed. It would be sad if the early years of wrestling history in New Zealand were not preserved as we had great history here in the days of holds and counter holds. Wrestling was a weekly event in the four main centres of New Zealand and town halls around the country were filled to overflowing on most nights. Gimmicks were out and the first gimmick wrestler to come here was "Whisker" Blake. He was soon tossed about by the whiskers but in general the American promoter Walter Miller saw that we had a high standard of wrestler come here for six months of the year in the winter season. They were hand picked, as Walter soon realized that New Zealand fans loved the skillful wrestlers who could apply holds and put on a good show for approximately one hour. We saw the best America had to offer, and there was no shortage of talent waiting to come here. They were great days when professional wrestling was considered a sport rather than an entertainment.

This is the first of two books on the history of New Zealand wrestling. The second book will cover the great wrestlers we had from America in the 1950s, 1960s, 1970s, and cover the long running "On the Mat show" weekly tv show, with Steve Rickard at the helm. Also the rise of Pat O'Connor from being a great amateur and British Empire Games medalist, to one of the world's great professional champions.

George Hackenschmidt and the early years

The earliest record I have of professional wrestling in New Zealand is a match in Auckland on June 20, 1894 between Donald Dinnie and P. White. Donald Dinnie was a prominent Scottish wrestler who had many contests on both sides of the Tasman. I have him on record as beating two opponents in one night in Auckland on June 4, 1896 when he defeated Tuohy and J.W. Sutherland. The same J.W. Sutherland won the New Zealand Middleweight title in August 1896.

Professional wrestling was very much alive in the late 1890s and the lighter weights also had New Zealand title fights; they also had professional champions of Auckland and other cities. The early 1900s saw wrestling at Caledonian sports meetings throughout the country and bouts took place in Dunedin, Masterton, Wellington, Palmerston North, Napier, Wanganui, Hawera, Gisborne and Invercargill.

I have a record of Cornish style wrestling in Epsom, Auckland in 1905, and a Cumberland style match in Masterton in 1910. Also on the same programme was a 'catch-as catch-can style' match, which was the main style favoured here.

The great world champion George Hackenschmidt came to New Zealand on two occasions, the first in 1904 when he beat the prominent Maori champion Moana Paratene from Gisborne. New Zealand's leading sports writer from the 1950s, Wallie Ingram, told me that as a small child he was taken by his father to see Hack beat Moana Paratene in quick time. Hack's next visit here and to Australia was in 1910.

This proved to be a longer visit and was mostly just exhibitions and feats of strength demonstrations. He brought a couple of his own sparring partners over with him in Alex Bain, a giant Scot, and Gunner Moir, a former champion boxer. He stayed from January 15 to 26 February and toured the entire country.

The Russian Lion
George Karl Julius Hackenschmidt

On the first day of his visit Hack won twice at His Majesty's Theatre in Auckland, beating his touring opponents Gunner Moir and Alex Bain on the same night.

Two nights later at the same theatre it was a repeat performance. In fact it was also a repeat on January 18 and 19 at the same theatre. On January 20 Hack beat C. Savoury and on the following two nights he beat Herb Hill and his two touring opponents respectively.

Following a one-day break, for travel purposes, "Hack" beat Moir in 2 minutes, 55 seconds, and Bain in 7 minutes, 52 seconds in Gisborne on January 24. On January 25 in Gisborne, Hack beat three opponents on the same night - Moir, Bayne, and Tawa Porter in 3 minutes and 55 seconds. Next it was Napier for a couple of exhibitions, Hastings, Palmerston North for two nights, Hawera, Masterton and Wellington for five nights. South to Christchurch for three nights, back to Wellington for a night, then Timaru, Oamaru, Dunedin for four nights, and finally Gore and Invercargill for two nights.

After Hacks visit wrestling was booming up and down the country, even though it was mainly exhibitions, fans had enjoyed seeing a world- class mat man in action.

George Hackenschmidt was also famous as a 'Strongman' and as a proponent on physical culture. He was a prize-winning gymnast as a teen and, as a 14 year-old, broke records for feats of strength including the pressing of a one pood weight 21 times with his left hand and 16 times with his right (Russian kettlebells are measured in poods and one pood equals 16kg).

I had the great pleasure of visiting the "Russian Lion" George Hackenschmidt at his home in West Norwood, London in 1960. He was still in terrific shape for a man of his years and still managed to do a little exercise. While I was visiting "Hack" he did twenty repetitions of rotating his leg over the back of a chair just to show me he could still do the exercises at 81 years of age.

Born in the Estonian town of Dorpat, which was then part of the Russian Empire, George first arrived in England early in 1902. When this broad shouldered young athlete first stepped ashore on British soil he was completely unknown, even though at this time he was the official heavyweight champion of the world. Wrestling was not a popular sport in Britain at this time, but Hack soon changed that. In 1904 at the Albert Hall he beat the American champion Tom Jenkins before 6,000 people.

Later that year Hack headed for Australia and New Zealand and he still clearly remembers these visits. He said the toughest of his Australian challengers was Clarence Weber, a fine all round athlete and the local champion. Hack told me that many of his opponents would come pleading to him before the matches to let them last a few minutes. But he told me he would never "carry" any opponent and most of his matches here ended inside a minute.

A rare postcard image of Hackenschmidt

After his tour of the Antipodes Hack headed for America, where he agreed to meet Tom Jenkins in a return match. After beating Jenkins and running up a string of victories in America and Canada, he returned to the British Isles. There he beat the Turk Madrali and many other famous names before returning to his home in Russia for a holiday. It was then back to the United States to prepare for the now famous matches with Frank Gotch.

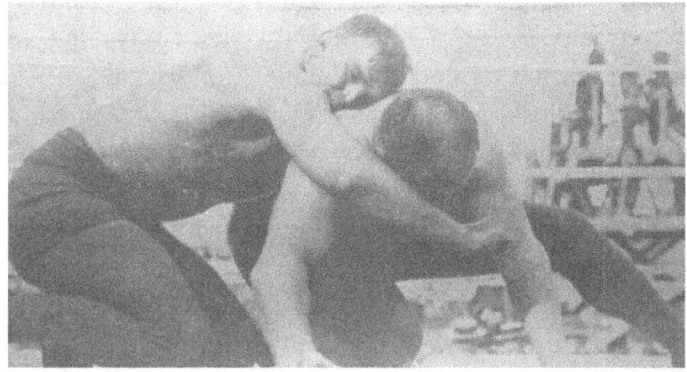

Most history books say that Hackenschmidt and Frank Gotch met twice; April 3 1908 at Dexter Park Pavillion and September 4 1911 at Cormisky Park (both in Chicago) and that Gotch won both times. Recent research indicates that they met several times over the years.

When I asked Hack who was the greatest he had ever met, he rated them in this order:
    1. Farmer Burns
    2. Tom Jenkins
    3. Frank Gotch.

Hack said his greatest regret was that he did not meet the great Indian wrestler "The Great Gama"; what a match that would have been.
Bert Assirati, the famous British wrestler and British champion for nearly twenty years, was rumoured to be after a match with Hack. But Hack said there was no truth in this, although Bert and his father had once come to visit him. Hack would have been too old, as Bert was only starting out in those days.
    During my visit Hack said that he had nothing to do with professional wrestling, and said it was all fake. "Not in my day", he said, when everything was genuine. Wrestling was televised twice weekly throughout Britain in 1960, but Hack flatly refused to watch.

Hack said he did however, take a great deal of interest in amateur wrestling and often went to amateur tournaments, where he sometimes presented the trophies.

When I went to visit Hack he had just returned from a lecturing tour of Germany. A lot of his time was spent travelling around the world lecturing on the mind and the body. Hack told me that he was interested in philosophy and that he spent his time meditating, not on his past triumphs, but on his own ideas for solving the problems of mankind.

Hack had many famous visitors during his later life in London. Among his friends was the late Bernard Shaw, who spent many a long and difficult session with him. Although Bernard could never quite follow Hack's reasoning, he was forced to admit that the man was no fool. Hack mastered several languages and wrote a number of books on wrestling, philosophy and physical culture.

Hackenschmidt in a typical 'Strongman' pose.

Among his many hobbies was gardening and he seemed to have a liking for apples. They were everywhere in his house, in bowls and even in drawers. I think it is safe to say that his eating habits did him no harm as he was in fine physical condition then at 81 (and he lived to be 90).

Hack's most popular book was the classic 'The Way To Live' and in it his last words sum up quite succinctly who he was:

"Throughout my whole career I have never bothered as to whether I was a Champion or not a Champion; The only title I have desired to be known by is simply my name - George Hackenschmidt".

Hackenschmidt's visits to New Zealand really sparked an interest in the wrestling game in the Dominion, much the same as Jem Mace's visits generated a wide-spread interest in boxing.

The author with George Hackenschmidt in the garden of his London home; April, 1960.

Walter Miller, who was later to become New Zealand's promoter for almost three decades, visited New Zealand in 1925 and beat Alex Anderson and R. DeCleene on the same night in Wellington. He was a fine wrestler and claimed to be World Champion in four different weight divisions.

Walter Miller (right) did great work promoting wrestling in New Zealand

Ike Robin and Stanislaus Zbyszko

Wrestling matches in the mid-twenties were very infrequent affairs in New Zealand. Perhaps a year or two would go by without more than a handful of bouts being staged. A big Maori boy was fast gaining popularity in the North of the country, and fans were eager to see Gisborne wrestler Ike Robin reach the top. In 1925 (at age 35) Ike beat Mahomet Ali Sunni for the vacant New Zealand heavyweight crown, and the same year in Auckland he beat Jack Clarke for the Australasian Heavyweight title.

The Maori Giant - Ike Robin (Ihakara Te Tuku Rapana)

Stanislaus Zbyszko first came to New Zealand in 1926. On that initial visit Zibby was in Auckland for one day only, and he agreed to meet any local wrestler on the night of June 22 1926. Thus was Robin, who had defeated Clarence Weber for the Australian title as well as his own

New Zealand crown, was brought in at short notice to Auckland to meet the former world champion. Robin matched the European in strength, if not so much in experience of the catch-as-catch-can style.

The bout was billed in error as being for the world title with Zibby the holder. But in actual fact Joe Stecher was the champion at this time (back in 1926 news travelled very slowly round the world and it was not uncommon for promoters to stretch the truth a little.) In fact the bald-headed Pole had first won the world title from Ed "Strangler" Lewis in 1921, and lost it back to Lewis less than a year later. He then regained the title in 1925 by beating Lewis' conquerer Wayne Munn, by two straight falls in less than 15 minutes, but had been defeated by Joe Stecher, "the scissors king," at St.Louis in May 1925. So when Stanislaus Zbyszko was in New Zealand, Joe Stecher was in fact the genuine world champion.

Promotional press for Zbyszko's return with Robin (New Zealand Sporting & Dramatic Review, September 6 1926)

These two mighty physical specimens met at the Auckland Town Hall, with Zbyszko standing 5ft. 8ins., and weighing 219pounds, and Ike Robin, over 6ft. weighed in at 259lbs. They wrestled 6 x 6 minute rounds, and over one thousand fans were unable to gain admittance.

The immense strength of the Maori was a revelation to Zbyszko. Try as he would, bringing into play all his ring-craft and cunning, Zbyszko could not pin the New Zealander's shoulders to the mat.

It was far from spectacular wrestling. On many occasions, when the Pole succeeded in bringing Ike to the floor, Robin would get onto his hands and knees, and no amount of strength could shift him. Zibby would straddle him and try all manner of holds, but he could not move this "Rock of Gibralter," as the billboards of the day labelled him.

The former world champion won on points, after no falls were scored. Zbyszko said after the match that Robin's strength was enormous. "The United States contains some excellent wrestlers, but there are none to compare with Ike Robin on that score. I would like to say that with two months proper training Ike would be a world beater."

Zbyszko and Ike Robin
The difference in size is staggering.

On his return to Auckland later the same year Zbyszko tangled with Robin on two more occasions. The first was on September 14 when another full house saw Robin on the attack almost throughout. There was much intense jockeying for position, but it was all strenuous work which kept the crowd closely attentive. On one occasion Zbyszko trapped Robin in a body-scissors but the mammoth Maori merely rose to his feet, lifted his opponent bodily, and shook him off like a dog.

Early in round five (this bout was scheduled for eight rounds) the visitor scored the first fall when he brought Robin down with a flying mare and pinned him with a quick body press.

A succession of fierce headlocks, which Zbyszko subsequently compared to those of his old rival, "Strangler" Lewis, kept the former champion on the defensive in the sixth, and the crowd almost lifted the roof off when the Maori threw Zbyszko out of a paralysing headlock and pinned him with a body roll. Referee Tennant Colledge was a popular official when he called the bout a draw at the end of the final round.

Ike, who was trained in the now outmoded Cumberland style, furnished a mighty resistance in each of three bouts with Zbyszko, losing the first on points, drawing the second, and dropping the third by one fall. In 22 rounds of wrestling, Robin conceded only two falls and secured one himself.

One of Ike's toughest opponents was Walter Miller, who in his day held four world wrestling titles - the lightweight, welterweight, middleweight, and light heavyweight championships (Walter spent six months in New Zealand every year as the booker of wrestlers to tour New Zealand). These two great mat men met four times with Ike winning three times and Walter once. Ike, however, was wrestling at around 18 stone, and when I met him he was 21 stone. He said Walter Miller was the most scientific wrestler he had ever met.

At the end of 1926 Ike Robin announced that he was retiring as the undefeated champion of New Zealand and Australasia. A man of deep religious beliefs, Robin was a lay preacher in his church. He was a tolerant kindly fellow whose athletic prowess was all the more amazing in view of this. Not only was he a champion at throwing the hammer, putting the shot, tossing the caber, and of course wrestling, but he was also a champion sheepshearer, and once claimed an Australasian record for the number of sheep shorn in nine hours.

Ike lived in retirement just outside Hastings, on the road to Clive in Hawkes Bay, and maintained an interest in wrestling for many years. I met him on one occasion in Gisborne around 1951, when he worked on the East Coast Commission. He was a charming man and I spent a couple of hours with him. My only regret is that I did not have a camera in those days. He told me that early in his long career he travelled to Australia to meet Ted Thye, and while there he was offered a boxing match against Tommy Burns. Ike turned the match down flatly, and said he had no intention of taking up boxing. The name of Ike Robin would have been a great draw against ex-world champion Tommy Burns.

Ike Robin: M.B.E.

Ike could have gone a long way in the sport, but he loved his homeland and didn't like travelling much. His trip to Australia was his only overseas trip. When he travelled to Wellington to receive his M.B.E. from the Governor General he found time to attend the Ken Kenneth--Al Costello match at the Wellington Town Hall. His only comment was that there was too much showmanship and not enough solid wrestling as had been the custom in his day. Ike Robin died 21 June 1968, he was 81.

Stanislaus Zbyszko was almost 48 years of age when he first appeared in New Zealand. Just two years after his performances in Auckland, Zibby retired from wrestling, but not before he engaged in a bizzare rematch with the Great Gama. The pair had first met in London in 1910 in the final of the John Bull World Championship. The 'match' lasted almost three hours, but there was little action and it was declared a draw.

The Great Gama

In the rematch Gama gained some semblance of revenge by throwing and defeating Zibby in 40 seconds.

Zbyszko never wrestled competitively again, but remained in the game as a talent scout. He discovered (and also trained) acrobatic gymnast Antonino Rocca, Johnny Valentine and Harley Race. In 1950, Zibby played a Greco-Roman wrestler in the movie, 'Night and the City'.

In his later years Zbyszko often said that wrestling had descended into just another form of showbusiness. Stanislaus Zbyszko died of a heart attack in 1967 - he was 88. Strangler Lewis called him one of the best legitimate wrestlers of all-time, and as a tribute, his surname was later adopted by contemporary star Larry Zbyszko.

Stanislaus Zbyszko (above left) John (Jack) Pesek in 1957 (*Photograph courtesy of Geoff Pesek.*)

On October 5 1928, Dave Scarrow from Raetihi won the first New Zealand amateur title at heavyweight by beating Billy Bayne. Bayne later competed with great success on both sides of the Tasman, but didn't get to wrestle for the Dominion Union. Lots of top boys were not used by the New Zealand Union as they lacked size and weight. Their policy was to bring in boys from the United States weighing 17 stone and more. Many of these same boys were huge favourites in Australian rings, and many settled there.

On November 28 1928, Billy Bayne beat an American Jack McLaughlan in his home territory of Te Awamutu. December 10 of the same year John Kilonis of U.S.A. beat Pat McCarthy, also of the U.S. in Auckland.

Above: *The front and back of a rare John Kilonis promotional card*

"The Terrible Greek" beat Mohammed Ali Sunni in Auckland on 14 January 1929 (his only recorded bout in New Zealand.) Kilonis later claimed the MWA Light-heavyweight Championship of the world.

In 1929 the Dominion Of New Zealand Wrestling Union was formed, and several rival groups that started up were short lived. It seemed wrestling was here to stay. Some leading American boys arrived here by ship in 1929. One was Clarence Eklund, the light-heavy weight champion of the world. Others to appear here were Tom Alley, Farmer Vance, George Walker, Maracci Gardini, Walter Johansson, and John Pesek, all top performers in the United States. The lighter boys were also active in 1929 - Dick Cameron, Charlie Pollard, Pat O'Brien, Ern Anderson and Billy Bayne. All were helping to draw the crowds.

Clarence Eklund (above) was one of the greats in the light-heavyweight division and was a genuine World Champion.

In the book 'Wyoming's Wrestling Rancher' written by Hazel Herberta Eklund Odegard, daughter of Clarence, there is mention of four matches in New Zealand. His match with George Walker was a draw and Clarence said he went close to being beaten by Walker. A week later in Auckland Clarence beat Farmer Vance in a world title defence. Another match with Farmer Vance is reported by the Otago Daily Times at the Kensington Drill Hall and Clarence won by two falls to one. In Christchurch Clarence beat Walter Johansson on points after each man scored a fall.

Maracci Gardini *(left)* had a few bouts here in 1929. Little is known about him. *The 1946 'Guide To Wrestling'* has the following piece: "One of Wellington's first matches saw Clarence Eklund and Tom Alley in action. Alley was the winner with his spectacular crucifix. A feature of the programme was a display of holds by Maracci Gardini, Wellingtonians did not know the difference between a headlock and a wristlock in those days."

Farmer Vance *(above)* was a top wrestler and billed here as *'The Light heavyweight Champion of Canada'*. His match with Eklund was fast and exciting. Round four was the round of the night. Vance came out of his corner full of fire and rushed in for his well known headlock. Five times in succession he put it on Eklund, and five times he swung his opponent round and over to crash him to the mat.

A HISTORY OF WRESTLING IN NEW ZEALAND

Pesek V Walker (above): Auckland Town Hall 1929.

Above (from back left): Unidentified - Al Haft (Prominent American promoter) - Unidentified - (front row from left): Tom Alley - John Pesek - Clarence Eklund - Joe Zigmund - George Walker. Aboard Union Steamship Company's 'Aorangi' 1928.

The 1930s

The 1930s saw wrestling off to a poor start with half full houses. But by the end of the first season houses were full and 1,500 fans could not get into the Wellington Town Hall on a Thursday evening, and the Government had made £2,000 in amusement taxes.

Some colourful characters arrived by ship in Wellington, when the S.S. Makura, from San Francisco docked in the capital city. On the passenger list he was plain Paul Aslan, but within a few weeks he was the most talked about man in the country and was more widely known as Kara Pasha "The Terrible Turk." With the coming of Pasha came the wrestling boom, and it blew away all doubts as to whether or not the sport had come to stay. From then on it was a case of being at the wrestling halls by 6.30pm or being turned away.

Kara Pasha "The Terrible Turk."

Professional wrestling was brought here to help foster the amateur side of the sport and they received a cut from the night's takings.

Some of the mat-men to come here during the 1930 season were Tom Alley, Walter Logan, Tom Ray, Scotty McDougall, Walter Hogg, Fred Ebert, Ted Thye, Tony Stecher, Howard Cantonwine, George Walker, Tom Lurich, Billy Edwards, Alex Lundyn, Ramzan Khan, Joe Stecher, Abe Coleman and George Kotsonaros.

In addition to the recently established Dominion of New Zealand Wrestling Union there were more and more associations springing up like mushrooms all over the country and they all affiliated to the Union. Small towns like Marton, Dannevirke, Stratford, Dargaville, Taumarunui, Waitara, Greymouth, Hawera and Thames, all promoted wrestling shows and the sport was thriving.

There was an opposition group early on and George Walker featured prominently in that, but the New Zealand Union were in the box seat. They told George his boys could only work for the union if they took out a licence for each wrestler as the union boys had to. George had his following and he brought in some top names from around the world. Some of the colorful characters who worked for George Walker were Tony Lamaro, Wong Buk Cheung (who also worked for the Dominion Union.) Jack "Rocky" Britton, Marin Plestina, Frank Judson, Louis Szabo, Frank Bronowicz, Tony Felice, Neil Rex, Harban Singh, Tiger Duala Singh, Roscoe Wahlberg, Fezal Mahomet, Billy Meeske, Peter Venter, Steve Savage, Hank Oswald, George Baumann and Snow Bartlett (another top Kiwi who made it overseas because the New Zealand Union didn't want him.) We also had Charlie Lowe, Syd Lack and countless others, some working for both the Union and for George's opposition group.

There was The Dominion Athletic and Wrestling Club, The New Zealand Wrestling Association, Pioneer Athletic Club, The National Sporting Club and others, and George had a finger in all of them. George said; "I disagreed with the tactics which were adopted by the Union and ultimately I refused to wrestle in matches under its control." George also stated; "Various bodies other than the wrestling union have from time to time endeavoured to promote bouts in New Zealand.

The police, however, made difficulties with permits for bouts other than those conducted by the Wrestling Union." This was back in 1932-3 and it appears that nothing much has changed to this day. Permits are still required for boxing and wrestling except for Vince McMahon's shows (WWE) which are now classed as sports entertainment.

GEORGE WALKER

George did later agree to work in with the Union and the rival bodies got together to lay a great foundation for the future of the sport in New Zealand.

New Zealand wrestling fans were very critical and selective, which meant only top mat-men were picked to spend several months here and then go on to Australia. The leading Americans all wanted to come here. When they left the country most were carrying a new wrestling bag; the old Gladstone bags made from the finest pig-skin were sought after here and were reputed to be the best in the world. (The Gladstone bag was used by doctors here for many years and sold in leather shops for around 25 shillings).

The wrestlers often brought their wives here and the four-week boat trip was an added bonus. The high standard expected from Kiwi fans meant we saw the best America had to offer. On more than one occasion a wrestler not up to standard was sent packing. There would be a small piece in the newspaper the following day saying a certain wrestler had been invalided home with a broken leg or such like. More often than not it meant that the wrestler was not up to the standard New Zealanders wanted.

The promoter expected them to wrestle for the best part of an hour to give the fans value for money and also to promote the amateurs. They loved coming here. The beautiful scenery and the New Zealand way of life appealed, but the number one criteria was they had to be able to wrestle for the best part of one hour or go at least six or seven of the eight round contests. Remember that in the U.S.A. many of the wrestlers only took part in twenty minute matches. Here they had to do eight eight minute rounds or the best of three falls, which usually meant an hour of grappling. The rest of the card here was put on by amateurs who wrestled from about 8:00pm till approximately 9:00pm. Then it was out to the foyer for a smoke and then back into the hall by about 9.15pm for the main event. The radio broadcasts usually started about 9.15pm.

George Walker was still promoting some independent shows in opposition to the Union, and these shows were well also attended.
The 1931 season got off to a flying start in Whangarei when George Walker beat Jack Higgins. George had by now decided to live in New Zealand. He was accepted as a Kiwi and became a firm favourite with wrestling fans, who all wanted to witness his back-loop-slam finishing hold. When George did this hold it was usually an early night.

Meanwhile Lofty Blomfield had won the New Zealand amateur heavyweight crown by beating Dave Scarrow in Wellington. He then headed off to Sydney and changed his name to Walter Browning. The young Lofty decided that as Lofty Blomfield, New Zealand amateur champion, he wouldn't create many waves in Australia, so he became a Canadian, and he never looked back.

1931 also saw some top talent in George Wilson, Stanley Pinto, Sam Burmister, Tom Lurich, King Elliott, Kara Pasha, Harry Demetral, Tom Alley, Scotty McDougall, George Pencheff, Rocky Marshall, Billy Meeske, and George Walker. Some of the smaller boys were also very active for a rival promotion and these included Anton Koolman, Billy Bayne and Tommy Bayne. George Walker won the New Zealand heavyweight crown, which in those days was fought between any of the visiting wrestlers. He was also claiming to be British Empire Champion.

Many more senior New Zealand wrestling fans will well remember Anton Koolman, especially those in the Wellington area, where the famous Koolman's Gymnasium was situated. All the top wrestlers, bodybuilders, boxers, weightlifters, gymnasts and general sports enthusiasts used to frequent this famous gym.

DAVE CAMERON

MATCHES HELD

Winner	Loser	Place	Date
Walker	Higgins	Whangarei	April 9
Walker	Lurich	Auckland	May 25
Walker	Limutkin	Wellington	June 1
Walker	Limutkin	Auckland	June 8
Pinto	Higgins	Auckland	June 15
Walker	Lurich	Hastings	June 15
McDougall	Alley	Auckland	June 22
Demetral	Higgins	Nelson	June 24
McDougall	Pinto	Dunedin	June 29
Alley	Limutkin	Christchurch	June 29
Pasha	Demetral	Wellington	June 29
Demetral	Limutkin	Stratford	July 2
Alley	McDougall	Auckland	July 6
Pinto	Demetral	Wellington	July 6
Lurich	Elliott	Hamilton	July 9
Pasha	Pinto	Christchurch	July 13
Demetral	McDougall	Dunedin	July 13
Alley	Lurich	Auckland	July 13
*Demetral	*Lurich	Hawera	July 16
Pinto	McDougall	Nelson	July 16
Walker	Pasha	Wellington	July 20
Buresh	Demetral	Auckland	July 20
*Burmister	*Pencheff	Masterton	July 21
*Pasha	*Demetral	Palmerston N.	July 22
Walker	Buresh	Christchurch	July 27
Pinto	Pencheff	New Plymouth	July 28
Pinto	Burmister	Hamilton	July 30
*Demetral	*Limutkin	Gisborne	July 30
Pasha	Buresh	Dunedin	Aug. 1
Alley	McDougall	Wellington	Aug. 3
Pinto	Walker	Auckland	Aug. 3
*Buresh	*Burmister	Invercargill	Aug. 5
Pencheff	McDougall	Stratford	Aug. 8
*Pinto	*Pasha	Wanganui	Aug. 8
Walker	Alley	Auckland	Aug. 10
*McDougall	*Lurich	Whangarei	Aug. 10
*Pencheff	*Buresh	Wellington	Aug. 10
Pasha	Demetral	Christchurch	Aug. 11
Burmister	Pencheff	Nelson	Aug. 13
Elliott	Higgins	Auckland	Aug. 15
Buresh	Limutkin	Westport	Aug. 15
Pinto	Walker	Wellington	Aug. 17
Marshall	Pencheff	Hastings	Aug. 17
Pasha	Limutkin	Blenheim	Aug. 19
Alley	Burmister	Gisborne	Aug. 20
*Pencheff	*Buresh	Hamilton	Aug. 21

9

From Wrestling in New Zealand 1931 season

A HISTORY OF WRESTLING IN NEW ZEALAND

Winner	Loser.	Place.	Date.
McDougall	Marshall	Auckland	Aug. 24
Alley	Pencheff	Stratford	Aug. 29
Pasha	Marshall	Dunedin	Aug. 31
Elliott	Lundyn	Wanganui	Aug. 31
Lurich	Alley	Auckland	Aug. 31
Pinto	Buresh	Nelson	Sept. 2
Marshall	Pencheff	Timaru	Sept. 2
Meeske	Burmister	Hastings	Sept. 4
Walker	Buresh	Auckland	Sept. 7
Pinto	Pasha	Wellington	Sept. 7
Burmister	Marshall	Christchurch	Sept. 7
*Pencheff	*McDougall	Hawera	Sept. 9
*Burmister	*McDougall	Hamilton	Sept. 11
Buresh	Marshall	Westport	Sept. 12
Walker	Pasha	Auckland	Sept. 14
Alley	Buresh	Nelson	Sept. 16
Pencheff	Elliott	Wanganui	Sept. 17
Alley	McDougall	New Plymouth	Sept. 19
Pasha	Buresh	Auckland	Sept. 21
Buresh and Pencheff declared no contest at Hawera, Sept. 23.			
Buresh	Elliott	Dunedin	Sept. 26
Alley	Pasha	Wellington	Sept. 28
Pinto	McDougall	Palmerston N.	Sept. 28
Meeske	Elliott	Invercargill	Sept. 30
Elliott	Marshall	New Plymouth	Oct. 3
Meeske	Buresh	Dunedin	Oct. 3
Elliott	Lundyn	Te Awamutu	Oct. 5
Pinto	Lurich	Auckland	Oct. 5
McDougall	Lundyn	Hastings	Oct. 9
Pasha	Marshall	Westport	Oct. 10
Alley	Meeske	Wellington	Oct. 12
McDougall	Elliott	Gisborne	Oct. 12
Alley	Buresh	Nelson	Oct. 15
Walker	Lurich	Hamilton	Oct. 15
Meeske	McDougall	Auckland	Oct. 19
Walker	Pasha	Wellington	Oct. 19
Meeske	Elliott	Hastings	Oct. 22
Alley	McDougall	Palmerston N.	Oct. 22
*Alley	*Lurich	Auckland	Oct. 27
Meeske	Pasha	Wellington	Oct. 27
Pinto	Meeske	Auckland	Nov. 2
Alley	Walker	Wellington	Nov. 2
Pinto	Lurich	Hamilton	Nov. 5
*Pinto	*Walker	Auckland	Nov. 9
Pinto	Meeske	Auckland	Nov. 16
Walker	Meeske	Auckland	Nov. 21
Pinto	Alley	Wellington	Nov. 23
Bayne	Koolman	Te Awamutu	Nov. 23
Walker	Meeske	Dunedin	Nov. 25

* Signifies a draw.

From Wrestling in New Zealand 1931 season

The cover of what was probably the first all-wrestling publication to appear in New Zealand. This copy previously belonged to famed boxing writer and historian Brian O'Brien (who once told me to stay away from wrestling as it was all rehearsed - though that was in the 1950s.) In the 1970s Brian was always chasing me for wrestling stories for his Sports Digest magazine, when the sport gained renewed popularity on TV.

I well remember my own trips to Wellington as a youngster and they were not complete without a visit to Koolman's to check out who might be training there. Anton Koolman was, without a doubt, one of the most skillful scientific wrestlers to ever set foot in this country. But he was too small for the visiting professional wrestlers' circuit and just far too good for most of them. It was a well-known fact in wrestling circles that the visiting professionals used to by-pass Koolman's gym, after first tangling with the master craftsman and getting a wrestling lesson into the bargain. The light-heavyweights, and even the heavyweights of the day, including Tom Alley, Dean Detton, Dr. Len Hall and so on, wouldn't have any part of this talented toe-twister. Even though Anton was only 5'6" tall, and weighed less than 160 pounds, he was arguably the best wrestler, pound for pound, that this country has ever seen.

(Above) the great Anton Koolman in his prime.

SHIMA RYGORO

Anton Koolman was very popular, not only in his gym (above - that's him in the ring in white), but also in the press. Anton's endorsements appeared to be quite valuable.

Koolman's Gymnasium in Wellington was a world famous gym used by many different sportsmen touring New Zealand. Every time I went to Wellington my first call would be a visit to Koolman's. Anton, an Olympic wrestler in Greco-Roman style, was always in the gym dressed in long white trousers and a singlet, giving instructions to weightlifters, boxers, wrestlers, gymnasts and other sports people. The gym was always a hive of activity.

Anton did get a break after a rival group to the New Zealand Wrestling Union started promoting bouts among the smaller men at Wellington's Winter Show Buildings. This was in the mid-thirties and Hughie Whitman, Jock Sinclair, Len Naylor, "Maltese" Joe Keotos, and New Zealand policeman King Elliot were some of his best-remembered opponents. The American imports used to dodge Anton because he was just too clever. They all knew his capabilities, as they worked out with him in his gym, but they weren't keen on meeting him in public.

When George Walker formed the Dominion of New Zealand Athletic Association, Anton was forced to don a mask and work on the undercard as the professional preliminary. Word of his ability quickly got round, and Anton found it hard to get top billing. The young Estonian originally came to New Zealand after cutting a wide swathe through amateur and professional wrestlers in Australia, but here the opportunities for making money were severely limited. He did however manage to secure a niche for himself as an instructor in later years.

One of the apples of his tutorial eye, Pat O'Connor, had moved from his blacksmith shop in Raetihi to be in the capital for some expert training. Pat of course, went on to become America's most sought after wrestler, and the first kiwi-born star to win the world professional heavyweight title. It is still a sore point with me that to this day Pat O'Connor has not been inducted into the "New Zealand Sports Hall of Fame."

Other Koolman boys to make good money in the hurley-burley of the American mat circuit have been Harry "Snow" Bartlett, who wrestled in the United States as Jack O'Reilly, and Dick Hrstich, who wrestled as Ray Gordon. Hrstich was the man who had preceded Pat O'Connor as New Zealand heavyweight amateur champion. Indeed those national amateur championships were dominated for many years by Koolman pupils, with such men as Leo Nolan, Bill Adams (father of professional wrestler Del Adams), Dick Godfrey, Sammy Bradley, Bob Hutchinson and Tom Anderson setting the pace.

Anton passed away on June 29 1953, but not before he had started his two young sons in amateur wrestling. Both Andrew and John appeared in amateur preliminary bouts in the Wellington Town Hall, and showed signs of the maestro's tuition. John later turned professional, and teamed with the New Zealand heavyweight champion Al

Hobman. John was huskier than his illustrious dad, and continued the family tradition, bringing back into circulation the Koolman Crab, a match winning hold embracing a full-nelson with sitback, which Koolman Senior had used to devastating effect.

Among Anton Koolman's coaching achievements, is a very rare book he wrote and published in 1938 titled "Koolman's Correct Wrestling". Included in this publication are a number of training tips, many of which are applicable not just for wrestlers, but for sports-people in general.

The following is the foreword from Anton's book, written by the master himself.

FOREWORD

"During the seven years of my stay in New Zealand I have received many letters from wrestling enthusiasts asking me to advise them as to what books they should procure to improve their knowledge of the game. Practically all the books that I have ever seen written in English are, more or less, endeavouring to teach a hold with one illustration. There are, of course, in America and other English-speaking countries publications on wrestling courses, which are seldom in book form. The wrestling holds and moves are so numerous that no book or course can demonstrate all of them, and to procure them all would naturally become too expensive. It is a fallacy to say that one cannot learn anything useful out of a book. Provided they have some little knowledge of wrestling they can learn quite a lot.

I, personally, have gleaned several good holds and moves from books through having some experience in the art of wrestling. Speaking of my own experience, I feel it fitting to mention to whom I am indebted for most of my knowledge of the game. First comes my schoolteacher, Mr. J. Leo, of Loksa, Estonia, who, with a Swedish drill instructor, used to make us perspire in the middle of winter when out in a snow-covered yard. After the drill we were paired off and made to "chest-hug," known as the "Cumberland" style of wrestling.

During the Russian Revolution, while serving in the Estonian navy, I got my first lessons in wrestling from Mr. Herman. Mr. Herman, seeing possibilities in me, took me to the Kalev Sports Club, Tallinn, Estonia, and put me under the wing of "Papa" Tomson. Kalev is noted as the Club where George Hackenschmidt, George Lurich, and Alex Aberg were moulded to become world's champions.

The present day world's amateur champion, Kristjan Palusalu, won the heavyweight in Greeko-Roman and catch-as-catch-can styles at the Berlin Olympiad and also European Championships at Paris in 1937, belongs to the same Club. (It is remarkable that for a little country like Estonia, with a population of less than one and a quarter millions, to produce so many worlds' champions during the past 35 years.)

The Kalev Sports Club is always after the best instructors. In 1922, Robert Oksa, who at that time was the world's best light-heavy weight amateur at Greeko-Roman style, was appointed as an instructor. Although "Papa" Tomson taught me a great deal, I can safely say Robert Oksa instilled more into me than all the rest put together. It is a sad loss to the game that Oksa never gave his knowledge to the world in book form.

Wrestling here and there during my sea travels, I eventually settled in Australia in 1925. Immediately I started learning the catch-at-catch-can style of wrestling with wrestlers like Ad Santel, with whom I practised scores of times, Mike Yokel, Martin Lydeck, Billy Meeske, Bert Potts, Dan Koloff and others, and who have helped me in learning the American style.

In addition to these two styles, I had the services of R. Shima, the jiu-jitsu expert, to teach me the art in my gymnasium in Wellington. From Shima I learned several moves that can be used advantageously in catch-as-catch-can wrestling. While Tiger Duala and Harbin Singh, the Indian wrestlers, were in Wellington,

I took particular notice of Indian styles while they trained in my gymnasium.

All told, I have had a thorough schooling in Greeko-Roman (sic) and catch-as-catch-can styles of wrestling, and more than a general knowledge of jiu-jitsu and Indian styles.

With this experience behind me, it was suggested that I should publish a book on wrestling that would be invaluable to young men aspiring to become wrestlers. The expense of such a publication was beyond me, but the idea occurred to me that if I could get a publication to issue a series of articles illustrated with photographs it could help considerably. The first man I saw was Mr. A. C. Geddes, Editor of the "Free Lance," Wellington (I take this early opportunity of thanking him most heartily for his kind consideration of this scheme), and he agreed to publish weekly illustrated articles in the "Free Lance" on wrestling, and afterwards kindly presented me with the blocks to do with as I pleased.

I have also to thank Mr. R. H. Parker, who helped me in many ways, and last, but not least, Mr. J. Casson, who straightened out all my "back-to-fronts" and "foreign knobs" that I wrote.

This book is only a part of the complete book that I intend to publish eventually. I hope that you who study it can understand all that you read and see in it. "

ANTON KOOLMAN.

Eighteen mat men from various countries arrived here in 1932, and in 1933 "Whiskers" Blake appeared and was a sensation with his whiskers. The first bearded wrestler to appear in New Zealand was lighter than most, but was a box office sensation when the fans found out he was getting tossed about by the whiskers. Not one of the great wrestlers to appear here, we later found out he was a geologist working in South Africa.

The famous Gladstone bag - a prerequisite for every wrestler on tour - seen here in an advertisement from the July, 1934 edition of Arena N.Z. Wrestling Weekly.

1934 saw some world class mat men arrive in Dean Detton and Gus Sonnenburg, both World Champions. The first Japanese heavyweight to apppear here in Oki Shikina, although a smaller Japanese boy had campaigned here when Rygori tested some of the lighter boys.

Oki was matched with Chinese mat man Wong Buk Cheung, and the 'House Full' signs were out when these two clashed. A mini war erupted when the Chinese boy clashed with the Japanese boy, and it was all good for business.

A HISTORY OF WRESTLING IN NEW ZEALAND

Chinese wrestler Wong Buk Cheung (above) seen here in a rare photograph from around 1934.

The first batch of visiting wrestlers for the season salute New Zealand with a Haka under the leadership of Harry Mamos. From left they are: C. Santen, O. Shikina, H. Mamos, F. Meyer, R. Michot (from '*Arena N.Z. Wrestling Weekly*' July 1934.)

Oki Shikina

Harry Mamos

Freddie Meyer

Rene Michot

Charlie Santen (above) on the cover of the June 1934 edition of Arena N.Z. Wrestling Weekly. Charlie was perhaps better known as Wally Dusek and was a cousin of the famous American family 'The Dusek Brothers' who were often referred to as "The Riot Squad".

Tony (above left) and Joe (above right) Stecher.

A rare autograph of Bulgarian great Dan Koloff who toured New Zealand in 1934.

George Walker (on the left) and Dan Koloff (on the right) ahead of their match at Wellington Town Hall 1934.

WRESTLING AGAIN.

A WIN FOR WALKER.

BLAKE WELL RECEIVED.

LOFTY AND BEARDED.

Roars of laughter greeted the opening of the 1933 wrestling season in the Town Hall last evening, when Whiskers Blake, 6ft 6in in height, failed to go the distance with George Walker. During the 22 minutes that the match lasted the elongated Blake displayed quite a few new holds and a luxuriant red beard, but neither his unknown holds nor his unusual facial decorations were of much use when Walker exerted his full strength. The attendance almost packed the hall.

Blake came to Auckland as a complete stranger. All that was known of him was that he was unnaturally tall, and that he sported one of those square beards that

SUPPLEMENT TO
N.Z. WRESTLING ARENA, JUNE 27th

EXTRA

WHY WALKER CAME BY PLANE

GEORGE WALKER flew down from Auckland! Everybody is asking how and why the wrestling hero missed and why was the match postponed from Monday? If he was indisposed on Monday is he fit to-day? Why was the postponement left so late? Is he fooling the public? Is it just publicity? What is the Union doing about it? These are the questions the wrestling fraternity are asking. The telephone has been kept busy.

THE ARENA SEEKS AN INTERVIEW

with the Chairman of the Wellington Wrestling Association. George Walker wrestled Patterson at Auckland on 19th to a draw. It was decided on the 20th that Walker should make his first Wellington appearance this season for the return match on the following Monday. Auckland, where Walker had been wrestling nearly every Monday released him for Wellington. He wrestled at Whangarei on Wednesday. Patterson reported at Wellington on Wednesday morning with an injured shoulder, the result of hammerlocks. Should the match at Wellington be postponed? Wait for a day. An urgent telegram to Walker on Wednesday: "Patterson slightly injured—don't come down till advised." On Thursday Patterson reported definite acceptance. Another telegram to walker: "Patterson all right—the match is on." On Monday (yesterday) at midday, a telegram was received from Walker, followed by telephone calls from our Auckland representatives, advising that Walker was indisposed and hadn't left. An inquiry was made of the doctor and he reported tonsilitis with slight temperature. The phones got hot. So did tempers!

Walker was distressed and agreed to come by 'plane that afternoon. Aero Club could not make it. Meantime Wellington practically sold all seats. A dozen more telephone exchanges. Could the match be postponed till Wednesday or Thursday? No! The Town Hall was not available. Somebody had it and, though only for a rehearsal, they wouldn't give it up. No one seemed to bother about the rent. **At midnight last night it was decided that Walker should fly down to-day. Well, here he is. WHO IS GOING TO WIN TO-NIGHT?**

An unusual and expensive way to get around New Zealand in 1933, but when the public want to see you.....

A HISTORY OF WRESTLING IN NEW ZEALAND

Dean Detton (above left) and Gus Sonnenberg (above right) and (below) Detton vaults over Sonnenberg's famous 'Flying Tackle'.

We were indeed lucky that the great Canadian mat man Earl McCready stopped by in 1935 along with Walter Miller, who became the promoter. Earl made 11 visits and proved to be the biggest star in New Zealand wrestling history. In total McCready had 416 bouts here and only 16 of those were losses.

Earl McCready and Walter Miller arriving in Auckland in 1935.

They put New Zealand wrestling on the map and - in Miller's case particularly - were responsible for the development of the sport in this country for over 25 years

When an Auckland radio station advertised pictures of Earl McCready and Lofty Blomfield, the response was overwhelming. You had to send in six pence in stamps, and over 6,000 of Earl and over 4,000 of Lofty, were sent out the first week. The radio station had to employ more staff to cope with the flood of letters.

Wrestling had by this time become a huge indoor sport with sellout attendances all over the country. Outdoor shows took place on weekends as well, usually on rugby fields with the ring in the middle of the field and a long way away from the action. I have 1930s pictures of outdoor shows in Westport, Greymouth, Nelson, Palmerston North and Auckland's Carlaw Park. 1936 saw a huge team come here consisting of 21 overseas stars including favourites Paul Boesch, Wee Willie Davis, Ed Don George, Jumping Joe Savoldi, and "Rebel" Bob Russell.

Wrestling fans were writing to wrestlers care of the Dominion office

Earl McCready (above left) and Lofty Blomfield (above right). These are the very same sixpenny photographs sold by the radio station. The picture of McCready was later signed in person by the man himself. The photograph of Lofty had a facsimile signature.

The small boy in the photo with Lofty is his nephew Peter.

in Wellington asking for autographed photos. In the 1936 season the New Zealand Union estimated that 20,000 letters were received from fans. I inherited some of the Dominion Union's material so I am able to show you how the letters went. Some had humorous paragraphs and here are a couple of examples:

A young lady writing to Sammy Stein from the South Island commences: *"I am a collector of professional wrestlers who come to our shores, so would you kindly send me a photograph of yourself."*

Then a young fan also writing to Sammy Stein asks *"Can you dropkick? I like flying tackles and elbow jolts and the Boston crab. I live on a farm and practice dropkicking on our cows."*

From a little fellow in Otago aged nine came the following: *"Do you think I could be wrestler. I wrestle a lot at school, and I eat a lot of vegetables, so that I will be strong enough to be a wrestler when I am big."*

Sammy Stein

The most controversial cover of this long-running wrestling guide (it went from 1936 to 1939 and then 1946 to 1952) featured Kara Pasha "The Terrible Turk". It certainly turned a few heads as it was widely available in the bookshops across New Zealand; very risque for 1936.

The standout match in 1936 was the long awaited match at Carlaw Park between Ed Don George and Earl McCready.

The outdoor match drew a huge crowd of near 12,000 and the fans saw one of Earl's rare defeats in New Zealand, when he lost by a fall after being thrown from the ring, hitting his head on a supporting ring post.

The years 1937 and 1938 also saw some class mat men here to test Earl McCready and our own Lofty Blomfield, who had refined his style after having at first proved too rough for New Zealand's high standard of grappling.

"Brother" Jonathan came in from Australia in 1938 for two matches, one at Carlaw Park. During his tour of Australia he had been taunting our champion Lofty Blomfield, and threatened to come over and destroy him.

"Ed" Don George (USA) was a world professional champion and also a top amateur.

Lofty was in peak condition and soon showed the talkative Mormon grappler who was boss. He offered him a return contest, but Jonathan was having no part of it, and after another losing contest at the Auckland Town Hall, to Ray Steele, the Mormon was on the first ship back to the United States. He did however take with him a Maori girl from Rotorua, who became his wife.

Mormon wrestler Brother Jonathan seen here with his young Maori wife (1938).

George Walker had decided to rejoin the New Zealand Union after spending several years running opposition shows and his eagerly awaited match against Earl McCready took place in Wellington. By this time George was no longer the grappler of old and, in what proved to be one of the shortest matches in New Zealand's wrestling history, he submitted to a hammer-lock in the first round and failed to come out for the second round. McCready had won what appeared to be the first shooting match in New Zealand, and there was certainly plenty of ill feeling between these two great Canadians.

The former great World Champion, Ed "Strangler" Lewis came in for six matches but was a huge disappointment and appeared well past his prime. The Wrestling Union took a stance and declared they would not promote wrestlers who were over the age of 50.

The signed photograph of Ed "Strangler" Lewis (above) was given to me by Ken Kenneth more than 25 years ago. Both wrestlers were great friends.

Early in 1938 before the season here got started Lofty was given the greatest match of his career when he took part in a World Heavyweight title match in Vancouver, Canada, against the champion Bronko Nagurski, also known as a famous footballer in American history.

The following report appeared in the Vancouver Sun on March 18:
"Lofty Blomfield, the gent from New Zealand didn't exactly lift Bronko Nagurski's world crown before a packed house at the Auditorium last evening. But he did take a pretty hefty swipe at it, and his buddies from down under need in no way be ashamed of him."

There was also wild excitement in New Zealand when word filtered through that Lofty had drawn his title match by putting on his octopus clamp in the last round to square the contest. The Wellington Sports Post devoted its whole front cover to Lofty putting his famed clamp on Nagurski. Lofty had improved out of sight and came home and drew his match with Earl McCready.

"Dirty" Dick Raines (also known as "Filthy" Richard) Ray Steele, Dean Detton, King Kong Cox, Prince Bhu Pinder, Rube Wright, and Chief Little Wolf all helped to keep the fans rolling in.

The 1930s were probably the most successful years in the history of the sport here, with the exception of the 1970s, when Steve Rickard's 'On the Mat' T.V. show had the whole country talking about wrestling again.

It was hard for locals to break into the sport here, as boys like "Kiwi" Kingston, Snow Bartlett, Ken Kenneth, Rod Douglas, and King Elliott found out, and all headed overseas to greener pastures.

These boys were all fine wrestlers, but the system in place at the time favoured bringing out a team of American boys, and using only Lofty Blomfield and later on Ken Kenneth. I recall "Kiwi" Kingston in England making a very good living from professional wrestling, and being a favourite all over Europe, despite being practically unknown in his own land. He was an Anton Koolman pupil, like many of the others who were not used here.

The 1930s were the days when wrestlers came to New Zealand and they all had their own pet holds. George Walker had his back loop slam, Lofty had his octopus clamp, Earl McCready his rocking chair splits etc. Over in Australia some of the pet holds were causing a problem, and our own Lofty Blomfield was the subject of a piece in the Sydney Morning Herald dated March 13 1937.

"BODYLINE" TACTICS IN WRESTLING, TOO."

"When the Leichhardt Stadium manager, Mr. George Jones changed his initial decision and agreed to Lofty Blomfield's proposal that the "dropkick" be eliminated from tonight's wrestling match, he took a stand that is sure to be the subject of vast discussion by the American Boxing and Wrestling Commissions.

Blomfield contends that the wrestling "drop kick" is in the same category as "bodyline" bowling - hence his protest.
Joe Savoldi, on the other hand, argues that the mode of attack has not been mentioned in the rules as foul tactics.
Australian's have the idea that everything goes in modern wrestling. After the original "Strangler" Lewis had nearly choked one of his opponents the "stranglehold" was barred."

I can only conclude that Lofty made the remark "tongue in cheek" as he had faced plenty of dropkick exponents in his own land. The referees in New Zealand were known to be stricter than in Australia, hence the many wild brawls that were common over there. The Chief Little Wolf - Dick Raines matches in Australia always ended in wild brawls, but it was rare for that to happen here. Lofty himself learnt his trade in Australia and on his return here he was always disqualified for being too rough.

Looking at pictures of some of the 1920s and 1930s wrestlers it was obvious some of them were getting on in years when they came out here, and were blocking the younger generation from entering the sport. It was often kept in the family much like it is today. John Pesek had his son Jack wrestling, and Dean Detton had his son Dory to follow in his footsteps. We were always told that an older wrestler had the knowledge and experience, and you didn't mature untill you were 45 or so, but it was pretty much a "closed shop" and very hard to break into the sport. I would liken it to an old boys club, but having said that there were some great shooters in the 1930s lineup. Guys like Ed Lewis, John Pesek, the Stecher brothers, Marin Plestina, Dean Detton,

Ray Steele and Earl McCready could hold their own in any company. A 1938 newspaper also questioned why Lofty Blomfield was the only wrestler competing against the American's:

"How long is Lofty Blomfield going to reign in solitary state as the only native New Zealander wrestling regularly with the imported Americans?

The only other New Zealander who has come anywhere near the eminence of Blomfield is Ike Robin, the giant Maori who was pitted against Stanislaus Zbyszko in 1926 at Auckland, and among his opponents in New Zealand and Australia was Walter Miller, the present manager of the Dominion Union's men. Incidentally, the fact that Miller, who was little more than half his opponents size, was able to handle Robin, should bring home to New Zealanders something that they are also inclined to forget-- when a big and a small man are opposed, the big man does not necessarily have matters all his own way."

During the 1930s wrestling was fortunate to receive great publicity in the newspapers. Every hold in a one hour match was written up in the following days paper. The Dominion Union put out a small booklet in 1931 titled 'Wrestling in New Zealand' and this was the first of many such items to come out. New Zealand even had its own weekly wrestling magazine, complete with coloured cover and sometimes a large coloured photo supplement. 'The Arena, New Zealand Wrestling Weekly', went through the wrestling season of about six months, and was around for several years. At the end of the 1934 season the Arena put out 'The Arena Wrestling Manual which demonstrated all the holds and had write-ups on the seasons mat-stars.

Tobacconists and barber shops had give away charts of all the wrestling holds for the radio listeners to study and kids were practicing the holds in the school play-grounds. One such chart had Lofty Blomfield on the cover putting the octopus clamp on Earl McCready. It was 'Popular Mat Moves - handy index booklet for Ringside Radio fans' and it sold for 1/- (one shilling). It opened up into a great chart of all the holds, and these would have been in many kids' bedrooms.

In 1936, the first of the yearly 'The New Zealand Sporting Life & Referee Guide To Wrestling' came out at 2/6 (a half-crown) a copy. It also had descriptions of all the holds and records of the previous season's wrestlers. It was a must buy for wrestling fans and I couldn't wait for the yearly edition to hit the bookshops. It went for eleven years with a break for the war years. The American wrestlers took home many copies and not too many of them are around today.

George Walker put out his own course, 'Scientific Wrestling', which was available in six parts from the George Walker School of Wrestling and Physical Culture. This was six booklet with a course on "how to wrestle" and went over pretty big in the 1930s. It was similar to Anton Koolman's book, but preceded the Estonian's efforts by a number of years. Amateur wrestling had a huge following in the 1930s and such books by the professionals were keenly sought after.

Bhu Pinder (above left) and Rube Wright - both enjoyed success in New Zealand wrestling rings in the late 1930s.

Original signed photos of Rollend Kirchmeyer (above left) and Joe "Kopack" Woods (above right). Below - a rare signature from "The Best Latin Heavyweight in the World", Ignacio Martinez.

PROGRAMME

ROYAL ALBERT HALL
Manager . . . . . REGINALD ASKEW

MAIN EVENT

WORLD TITLE ELIMINATION CONTEST

8 (8-min.) ROUNDS. 2 OUT OF 3 FALLS

EARL
McCREADY
BRITISH EMPIRE CHAMPION   16 st. 12 lb.

v.

RUBEN
WRIGHT
UNITED STATES   18 st. 3 lb.

SEMI-FINAL

Contest for the Light-Heavy-weight Championship of the British Empire

5 (8-min.) ROUNDS. ONE FALL FINISH

LOUIS PERGANTIS
SOUTH AFRICA

v.

CARL VAN WURDEN
CANADA

Page Eight

WORLD TITLE
Elimination Contest
Catch-as-Catch-Can
WRESTLING

TUESDAY, AUGUST 23rd, 1938

PROGRAMME ONE SHILLING

PRINTED BY
FLEETWAY PRESS LTD. 11/21, EMERALD STREET, LONDON, W.C.1

(Above) pages from the programme for Earl McCready's World Title elimination fight against Rube Wright of the USA at the Royal Albert Hall in August 1938. The match was of particular significance as it was the first ever televised wrestling match. The same event is often mistakenly recorded as taking place at Crystal Palace.

This copy of the programme was sent by McCready to Wally Ingram in Wellington. Ingram was a famous radio presenter who loved wrestling and had a good deal of time for its participants. Wally actually went to Te Harpara school in Gisborne with Tom Heeney.

One of the most popular wrestlers to ever visit Australia and New Zealand was Chief Little Wolf, who for over twenty years thrilled mat fans with his wild style of grappling.

Born Ventura Tenario in a small town named Hoehme, which is situated about twelve miles from Trinidad in Colorado, the Chief's mother was a full-blooded Navajo Indian and his father was half Navajo - half Spanish.

Although Little Wolf was three-quarters Navajo, he couldn't really be classed as a real Navajo chief, because only full-blooded braves and warriors can achieve that rare honour. However seeing Little Wolf was showing such great promise as a wrestler, his tribe dubbed him Chief - an honorary title he never ever lost.

Standing only 5ft. 8 3/4 inches and weighing in at 252lbs. the Chief had the fantastic chest measurement of 61inches and a 45 inch waist. He's been called square set, chunky, roly-poly, sturdy and sometimes round.

Chief Little Wolf

As a youngster the Chief was always good at sport, particularly track and field. His great idol was Jack Dempsey, 'the Manassa Mauler', so it was no surprise when he became interested in boxing. As a light welter he had six fights under the name of Young Dempsey and came second in the Inter Rocky States title which attracted about 100 budding stars from around Colorado, Utah, Wyoming, and New Mexico. A little later he became interested in wrestling and there was a guy promoting in Trinidad. One of his stars was Ben Bolt - a Sioux Indian. "I decided I had to watch this guy in action" said the Chief, and "that's when the wrestling bug really hit me. And the wanderlust, which has stayed with me ever since."

After wrestling in the lighter weight divisions for several months, the Chief made such rapid progress in the grappling game that he was matched with Gus Kallio, the middleweight champion of the world, who was known as the "Mighty Finn".

After three and a half hours of solid wrestling Kallio was declared the winner by one fall to none. "No grappler before or since had the endurance of that guy. He came in with elbows forward throughout the bout and among other things cut my eyebrows to ribbons," declared the Chief.

The Chief was only 19 years of age when he met Kallio and rated this the outstanding match of his long career. He was one of the few men to have battled for the World Wrestling Championship in four divisions, welterweight, middleweight, light heavyweight and heavyweight.

Another match that stands out in the Chief's memory was his World Heavyweight Championship clash with Danno O'Mahoney before a record crowd at New York's Yankee Stadium. O'Mahoney had only recently lifted the crown from the "Golden Greek". Jimmy Londos, and was in great shape. The bout started at 9:45p.m. and when midnight came the score was one fall each. The curfew was midnight, otherwise the match would have continued untill a winner was decided. The rematch was in Chicago and this time O'Mahoney won by two falls to one.

Other big names the Chief met in his long career were Jim McMillan, Ray Steele, Ed "Strangler" Lewis, and flying tackle expert Gus Sonnenberg.

Another tough match took place in Denver where he faced two-ton Tony Galento. He was the cigar-smoking, beer-swilling Italian, who once fought Joe Louis for the Heavyweight Championship of the World. Tony was beaten by two falls to none, thanks to the Indian Deathlock, the hold which the Chief made famous throughout the wrestling world.

Tony was annoyed after the bout and declared that in a boxing match he would flatten Little Wolf in four rounds. The challenge was accepted and at the end of the fourth round both men were still on their feet and slugging away at each other.

One of his other ring rivals was the equally colourful Texan, Sky Hi Lee, "a mighty big fella" according to Chief Little Wolf. Little Wolf beat Lee on three occasions and lost to him once.

Perhaps his biggest roughhouse ever was in Melbourne back in 1953 after the Dick Raines - Don Beitleman bout. The Chief was sitting at ringside as a spectator and wasn't too happy about it either, as he had been passed unfit by the doctor. His opponent was to have been "Dirty" Dick Raines. In the sixth round after referee Bonnie Muir had disqualified both men, the Chief jumped in the ring and had a go at Raines. He snatched the ring microphone from an astonished broadcaster and explained to the fans that he was supposed to wrestle Raines, and then promptly challenged Raines to meet him the following week. This match ended in a draw after Raines obtained a fall with his backbreaker and the Chief equalised in the final round with the deathlock. The Chief learned the Indian Deathlock from the way Geronimo (the big tough Chief who hated the palefaces) used to torture his arch - enemies. Geronimo would take his captives, have them stripped, then set a stake pole on top of an ant-hill and the legs of the prisoner would be entwined around the stake. The more he struggled, the greater the pain. The body was then covered with honey and the ants did the rest.

The Indian deathlock is identical to this method of torture, except the leg takes the place of the upright stake.
With this hold the Chief has broken the legs of six wrestlers, among them Man Mountain Dean, Dean Detton, Joe Savoldi, and Sammy Stein.

During World War two the Chief found himself in the uniform of Uncle Sam's army and his particular job was instructor in a Commando unit. He was invalided home from Sicily but finished up a Provost Marshall at the infamous stockade in Los Angeles, California.

Chief Little Wolf with yours truly (above) and (below) the Chief's daughter Markeeta - who was actually a pretty good singer who did well on the cabaret and night club circuit.

MARKEETA LITTLE WOLF

When the Chief finally retired he toured Australia and New Zealand demonstrating his famous deathlock, and gave talks on self defence and Indian folk lore. The Chief took such a great liking to Australia that he settled in Melbourne and for many years was the local favourite against the visiting foreign wrestlers who invaded the country each season.

After visiting the Chief in a Melbourne hospital in 1969 and 1970 we became firm friends, and I used to get regular reports from the hospital on his condition. The Chief had suffered several strokes which had left him paralysed down one side. Brother Petersen, the Mormon missionary who looked after the Chief, wrote to me regularly and told me of their plans to one day visit the Mormon temple in Hamilton, New Zealand.

Several years passed and in 1978 I received a letter to say meet us at Auckland airport. I arrived at the airport and the Chief was very pleased to see me again. I brought them home to see my wrestling history and the Chief was pretty impressed that I had a photo of his three wives. I had to carry him up stairs to our house as he had got very frail and was only half his original weight.

    I drove them over the harbour bridge to visit my Dad, who had also visited the Chief in his hospital bed in Melbourne. My Dad remembered the Chief from the radio days before the war and was delighted to see him again. Then it was back to see more of my collection which the Chief enjoyed. Around midnight I suggested the Chief should stay the night, but he insisted he was booked in at the temple in Hamilton (this was more than two hours drive). I should add it was a wet Auckland night when we got in the old Volkswaggon and headed for Hamilton. Heading down towards the Bombay Hills we got a puncture and it was out in the rain to do a quick tyre change. After a short stop we were away again and about half way to Hamilton we got another puncture. I duly jacked up the car, took the rear right wheel off, explained to the Chief and Brother Petersen that I would have to get the wheel back to an all night service station that we had passed some minutes earlier. Bowling the wheel along the main road in pouring rain was no fun and I was surprised when a police car pulled up behind me. The policeman was happy to take me to the Service Station where he waited while I got the puncture mended. He drove me back to where we were parked and helped me put the wheel back. When I got back in the car the Chief presented me with the Book of Mormon, which he and Brother Peterson had autographed for me.

    From then on it was a nightmare trip as I got lost and could not find the temple and the rain was still pelting down. I drove around Hamilton in the early hours looking for someone to point me in the right direction but couldn't find a soul.

We talked of the great wrestlers that came to New Zealand and I recall the Chief saying Earl McCready was the greatest he met. We also talked of the New Zealand beer. The Chief said if he hadn't drank so much New Zealand beer he would be in better shape. He had a lasting injury from a match with McCready where had lost a rib. I well recall the Chief telling me to feel where the rib should be.

It was almost daylight when I got the two men to the temple, so when I arrived back in Auckland in peak morning traffic I promptly phoned work and said I was sick. A few days later the two boys came back for another visit and them headed to California, where the Chief had many contacts.

My dad Rev. Ian Cameron, puts a wristlock on the Chief (above) and (left) the Chief, Brother Dayne Petersen and my son Paul. The top photograph was taken at my dad's home in Lynfield, Auckland and the one on the left at my home in Auckland (both 1978).

Chief Little Wolf had a holiday in the States and then returned to his hospital bed in Melbourne. A few years later I received a phone call from the Chief to say he was in Auckland on a stop over and was heading back to the USA. He told me he wanted to go home to die in the US and he would not see me again. Quite a sad moment for me and

I could tell the Chief was tearfull also. That was my last contact with Chief Little Wolf and I will never forget those great memories.

Chief Little Wolf passed away in 1984 in Colarado. U.S.A.

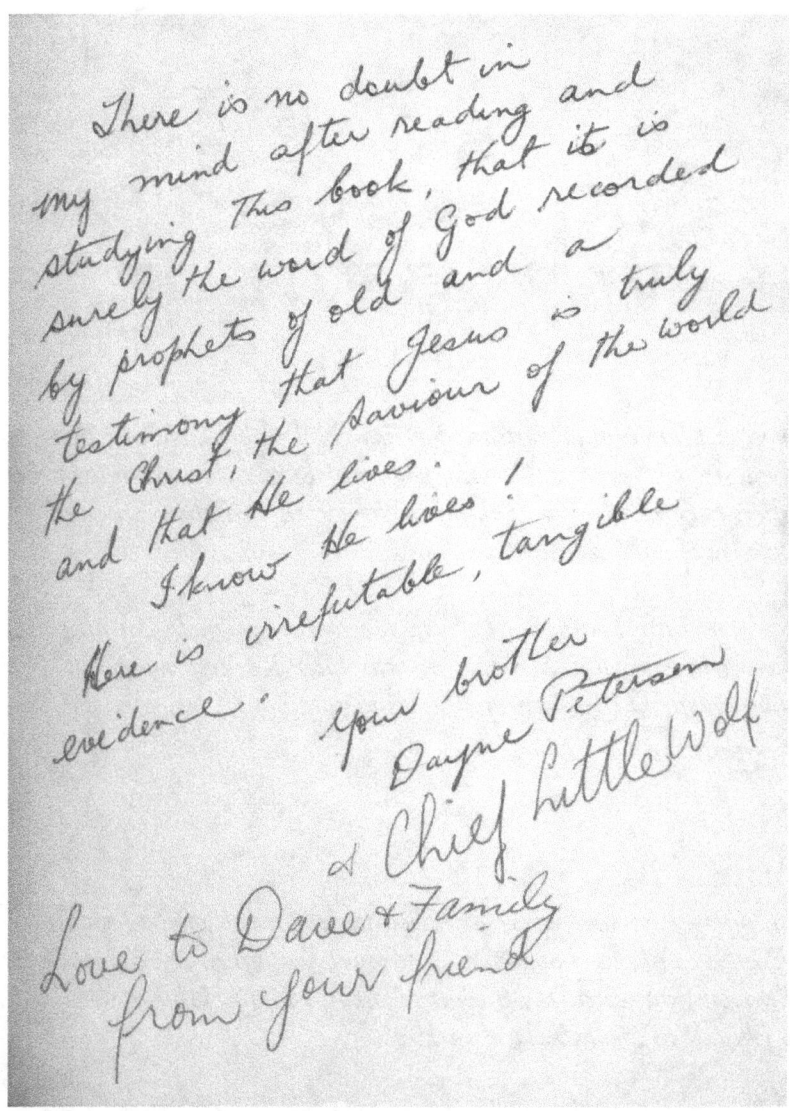

Brother Petersen and the Chief presented me with a signed copy of 'The Book of Mormon' (above) after our Hamilton adventure.

RAY STEELE

(Above) a promotional postcard for Ray Steele who was born Peter Sauer in the town of Norka, a German colony of Russia. He was one of the best wrestlers to come to New Zealand in the 1930s and always showed a great knowledge of holds and counter holds.

It was not until 1940 that he won the world crown by pinning Bronko Nagurski in St Louis, Missouri. A year later Ray lost the crown back to Bronko Nagurski in Minneapolis, Minnesota.

(Facing page) Farmer Vance demonstrates the finish of the famous "Wing Lock" on an unknown opponent. The photo was taken in Anton Koolman's Wellington gym (circa 1930). Vance lost in a championship bout to Clarence Eklund in New Zealand in 1929.

Billy Meeske (Australia) holds Tom Alley on the mat with a Japanese wristlock - Wellington Town Hall December 9 1931.

Alley 13st. 10lb. won from Meeske 12st. 3lb. The contest was to have been for the world light-heavyweight title, but Alley weighed above the stipulated weight of 12st. 7lb, so it became a non-title affair. Alley was on top to the last round and was given the decision.

Wellington Town Hall: October 19 1931

Before the match referee Jack Lack gives Walker and Pasha final instructions (above). Second round (below) Pasha tries for a "Boston Crab" but Walker was able to kick himself free just in time.

Action from the match between Tom Alley and Scotty McDougall: Wellington Town Hall August 3 1931.

Top: Tom Alley submits in the 3rd round to his own famous hold the "Crucifix" - the referee has just broken the hold. Below: McDougall does all the attacking in round 3 and nearly obtains a "key lock" - it was not fully developed however and Alley broke free with the aid of a "splits".

Top: Alley punishes McDougall in round 5 with a "short-arm scissors" which he finally worked into a "Japanese arm-bar" to win the match.

Below: McDougall submits to a "Japanese arm-bar" in round 5; thus giving Alley the match.

LAST NIGHT'S CONTEST
MATCH DRAWN

"Although lacking a good deal of the spectacular which some matmen manage to make their work, the wrestling match in the Town Hall last night between Stanley Buresh and George Pencheff was strenuous and keenly contested. Evenly matched in strength, the pair did eight rounds solid, and for the most part, straight wrestling, at the end-of-which, no falls being recorded, the bout was declared a draw. Most of the evening the wrestlers were on the mat struggling hard, but they did not neglect opportunities to introduce just a touch of the showmanship which adds variety and interest to the proceedings. Nevertheless it must be said that this was not overdone and the instant obedience of the contestants to the commands of the referee was one of the features of a clean, hard-fought match."

Wellington Evening Post: August 11 1931, Page 12.

(Opposite - top) Pencheff putting a "Head Scissors" on Buresh and (opposite below) Buresh punishes Pencheff with a "Toe Hold".

(This page) More action from the same match as (top) Pencheff tries to turn Buresh over for a "Boston crab" and (below) Pencheff stands Buresh on his head and bumps him on the mat several times in round 6.

Pinto and Pasha, two of the greatest wrestlers and showmen ever matched in Wellington - above is a typical example of their amusing antics in the ring. (Below) hard work on the mat in the second round as Pinto works on a "Headlock".

(top) More bi-play as Pasha manages to stand up in a "Head Scissors". Wellington Town Hall September 7 1931 (referee Jack Lack).

Anton Koolman gains first fall in a prelim match with a "Full-Nelson" and a "Reverse Boston", the opponent is Billy Bayne of Taumarunui (below). Koolman won two falls to none in the third and fourth rounds. Wellington Town Hall September 7 1931 (referee is Jack Lack).

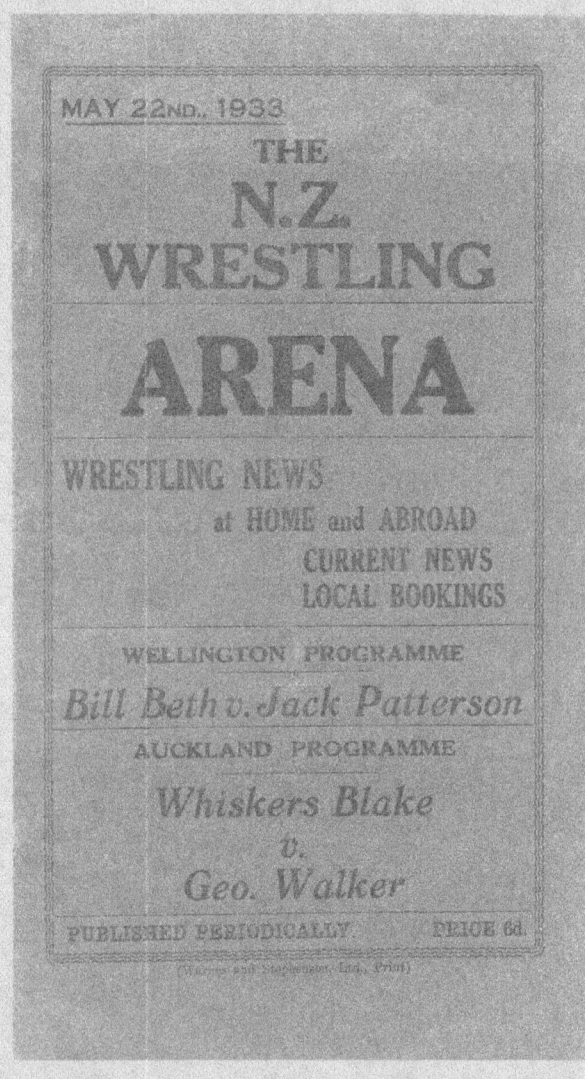

The second issue of 'The NZ Wrestling Arena' from May 22 1933. The first edition was initially sold in Wellington, but a high demand meant that the publishers brought out a second edition nationwide. The booklet contained all of the matches and results from across New Zealand along with international news. The popular publication was put out with the approval of the New Zealand Wrestling Union.

The Arena changed its look just two months later.

By October the Arena had changed its look again. The format was larger and the page count increased from 12 to 16.

The Arena changes its look again (July 1934). There are still 16 pages, but the number of action photographs increases, as does the international reporting. There is even news from the boxing world (Dean Detton appears on the cover).

'The Arena Manual' from 1934. The manual was - according to the publisher - produced for the radio-listening fans at a significant cost. Fans were listening to the matches on the radio in New Zealand and Australia and the publication assisted in their appreciation of the ring action by illustrating all of the main holds. The Manual claimed that wrestling was (at the time) "the biggest attraction of all indoor forms of entertainment."

The great Jack Dempsey (right) was a good friend to many professional wrestlers, including Chief Little Wolf and Jack Claybourne. The "Manassa Mauler" was also guest referee for many wrestling bouts.

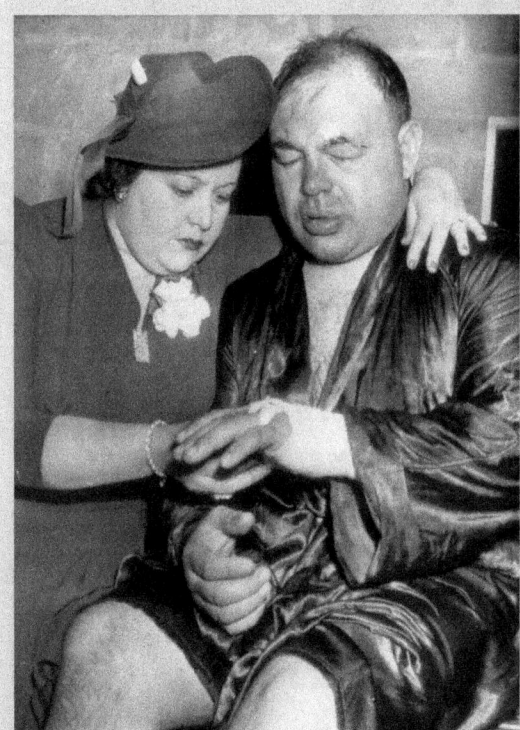

Two-Ton Tony Galento - heavyweight contender in the 1940s (left) once had a boxing match with Chief Little Wolf.

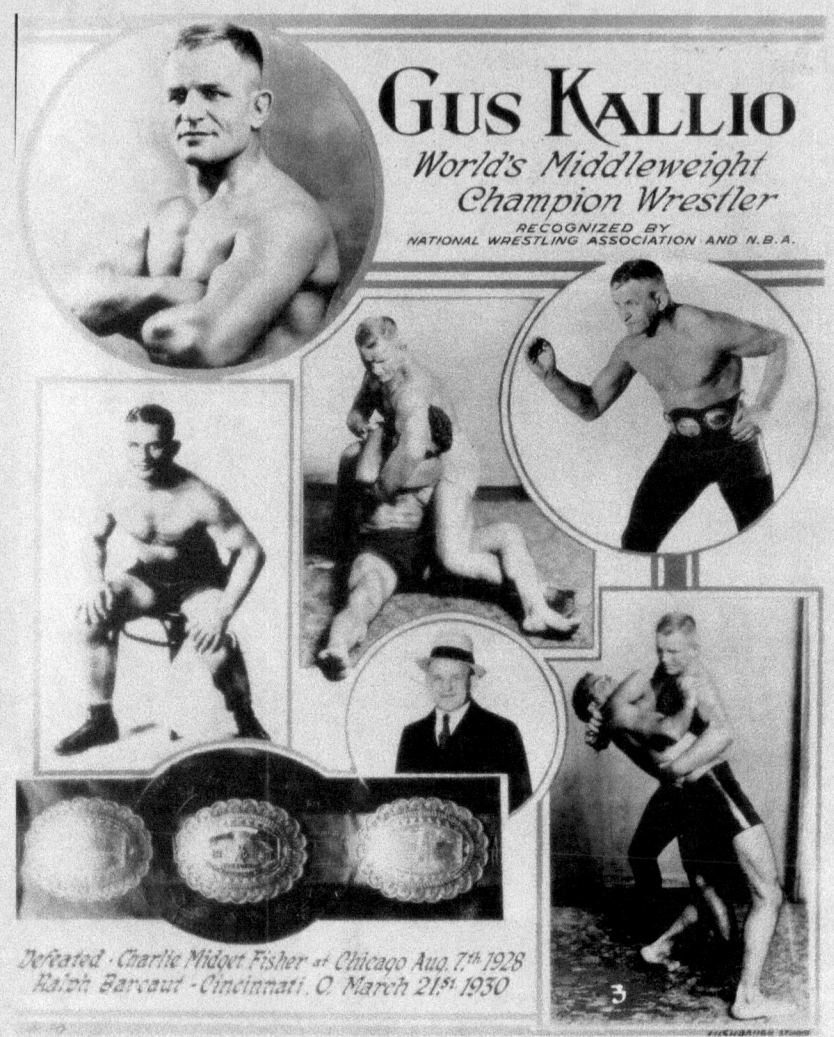

Welterweight and middleweight world champion Gus Kallio (above). Kallio wrestled Chief Little Wolf - amongst many others - and the Chief told me that Kallio was the greatest wrestler he ever saw or wrestled against. Ken Kenneth (who gave me this photograph) backed this up by telling me that the Finn was the best wrestler he ever saw - at any weight. High praise indeed - Kallio must have been something to see.

The 1940s

During the mid 1940s I became a boxing and wrestling "nut" and things are no different today, some seventy years later. Professional wrestling had some quiet years in the early 1940s with many of the boys away at war. Lofty Blomfield was one of the first to enlist. After several months hard training in camps around Auckland and a spell at Trentham Military Camp (under the control of Regimental Staff Sergeant Major Douglas) Lofty sent off to Egypt.

Lofty in a photo he signed and presented to Wally Ingram before going off to Egypt (circa 1940).

The smaller team in 1940 consisted of Lofty, Chief Little Wolf, Joe Corbett, Dick Raines, John Katan, Earl McCready, Dan O'Connor and Harbin Singh. Ken Kenneth was wrestling but had not reached the standard needed to compete against the Americans. Ken was wrestling boys like Mark Maich, Frank Boric, Bill McIvor and Dr. Barto Hill, an American serviceman who spent some time here.

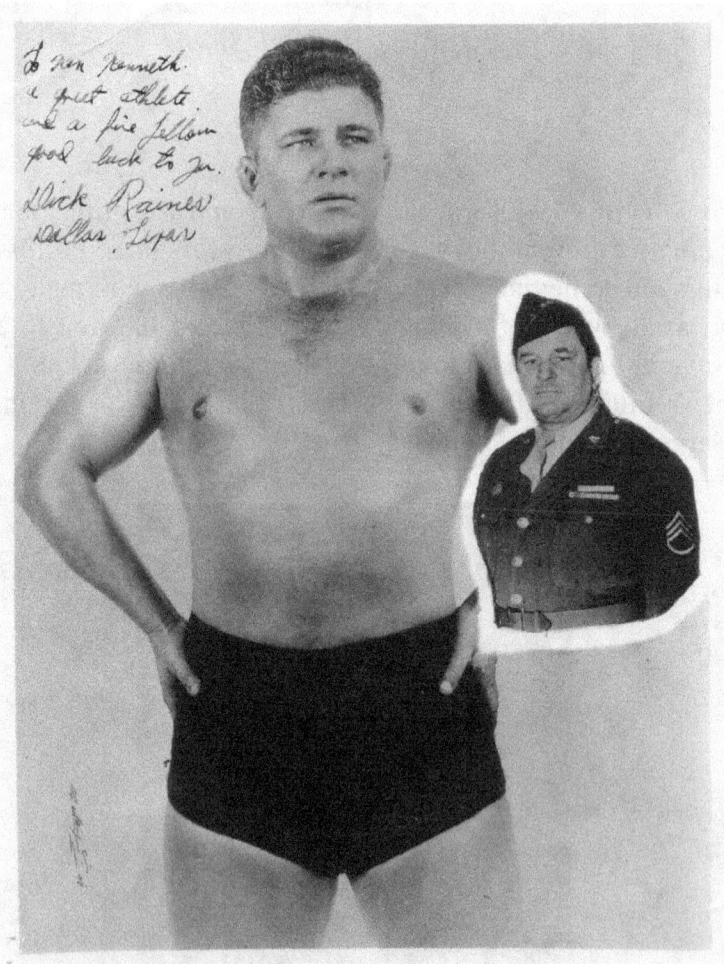

Dick Raines in a photograph he gave to Ken Kenneth in 1940. Inset is Dirty Dick in his military uniform as a US serviceman.

A HISTORY OF WRESTLING IN NEW ZEALAND

Ken Kenneth (left) as a young, keen amateur wrestler. Ken used to go around the Auckland gyms looking to work out with the visiting American professionals.

Ken Kenneth

In his professional wrestling days in the 1940s. Ken signed this one for me during one of our many meetings.

Frank Boric (top left) and Carr Gates out pig-hunting (top right) and (above) "Dirty" Dick Raines demonstrates his "Back-breaker" move on Ken Kenneth at an Auckland North Shore primary school (circa 1940).

The following four pages are an original programme from September 1940.

AUCKLAND WRESTLING ASSOCIATION (Inc.)
WRESTLING NEWS and OFFICIAL PROGRAMME

No. 16   MONDAY, SEPTEMBER 9th, 1940   New Series

SERGEANT-MAJOR BLOMFIELD

TOWN HALL, MONDAY, SEPT. 9th, 1940

Sergeant-Major
LOFTY BLOMFIELD
(British Empire Champion)

v.

JOHN KATAN
(Challenger)

DEMAND
Monarch
Real Pork Sausages
GRILLED FOR BREAKFAST

They give HEALTH and STRENGTH for any sport

WRESTLING NEWS   Monday, September 9, 1940.

You will be heartily welcomed at the
NAVAL & FAMILY HOTEL
Matt Brodie   •   Proprietor

Lion Ale on Tap

F. W. LUCAS LTD.

THE MEN'S OUTFITTERS

123 QUEEN STREET, AUCKLAND

Consult us for all Men's Apparel

- OVERCOATS
- LYNX SUITS
- SHIRTS
- HATS

in fact everything for the well-dressed man at prices to suit all pockets.

'The Sportsman's Rendezvous'

below Bank of New Zealand.

---

8 p.m. AMATEUR BOUTS

R. Williams, 11.4 (Surrey), v. K. McLeod, 11.0 (Lynndale).

L. Hawkins, 9.4 (Y.M.C.A.), v. C. Hammond, 9.2 (Lynndale).

J. Vinac, 12.9 (Auckland), v. H. Young, 13.6 (Surrey)

B. Waugh, 9.9 (Surrey), v. J. Monaghan, 10.3 (Auckland).

T. Harvey, 9.4 (Auckland), v. W. Jackson, 10.0 (Y.M.C.A.).

J. Wright, 10.8 (Auckland), v. E. Warner, 10.5 (Lynndale).

Referee : MR. F. MURPHY.

8.30 JUNIOR PROFESSIONAL BOUT

5 FIVE-MINUTE ROUNDS

BILL McIVOR
v.
FRANK BORIC

Referee : MR. J. McLEAN

SUMMIT BRAND

Shirts and Pyjamas

Shaped Garments—Cut to Fit.

Monday, September 9, 1940.   WRESTLING NEWS   3

From TIP to TOBACCO....
DE RESKE
ARE SO MUCH BETTER!

---

9 P.M.

MAIN EVENT
8 EIGHT-MINUTE ROUNDS
LOFTY BLOMFIELD
v.
JOHN KATAN

Referee: MR. J. McLEAN

PAUL BOESCH

Paul "Bombshell" Boesch, who has been in Australia, passed through Auckland on his way home. Boesch said he was sorry he had to miss a tour of New Zealand; but as his mother, who he had not seen for two years, was very ill, he had decided to go straight home.

Boesch has been asked to pay a return visit to Australia next season.

You'll like it BETTER, it's BETTER FOR YOU!

LION ALE

Brewed at the "Lion" Brewery, Khyber Pass.

AUCKLAND LAUNDRY CO. LTD.
——— SURREY CRESCENT ———

ARE ALSO QUALITY DRY CLEANERS

Telephone 26-632

PROMPT DELIVERY.   Our "Vanman" will be delighted to collect your **Dry Cleaning** with your laundry parcels.

WRESTLING NEWS   Monday, September 9, 1940.

BLOMFIELD v. KATAN

Although John Katan naturally attaches considerable importance to the Empire title, which he came all this way to win, the matter of beating Blomfield for his own personal satisfaction weighs with him equally heavily.

He has been muttering about his match with Blomfield ever since he lost the title and not until he has had a chance to show that things should have happened differently will he be anywhere near satisfied.

Last Monday at Wellington, Katan went the full distance with Blomfield but had to be satisfied with a draw after each man had taken a fall.

Katan is certainly a determined fellow when he sets his heart upon something. He chased McCready out here in order to get a bout for the title, he threatened to go home if he did not get a chance to turn the tables on Blomfield, and, when an unavoidable delay occurred, prolonged his visit so that there would be no excuse for his being given the slip.

After the Wellington bout Katan still claims that he has precedent over McCready as his fellow Canadian had his chance and failed at Auckland last week.

As Blomfield was agreeable to meet Katan again, the Dominion Union has given Katan another chance and Auckland fans a match in which Blomfield and Katan can be depended upon to give them plenty of thrills and brilliant wrestling for their money.

In the junior professional bout, Bill McIvor, who has been off the scene for some weeks, will make a welcome reappearance in a bout with Frank Bovic, the popular Dalmatian wrestler.

EMPIRE WRESTLING
BLOMFIELD RETAINS TITLE

By holding the challenger, John Katan, to a draw, one fall each, Lofty Blomfield retained the British Empire wrestling championship as a result of a remarkably fast and vigorous bout. Katan took the first fall with a jack-knife in the fourth round. Blomfield drew even with an octopus clamp in the sixth. The contest was easily the most exciting seen in Wellington. Every seat in the Town Hall was taken and scores watched the bout standing. Scenes of hysterical enthusiasm marked the falls and the ultimate decision.

BON VOYAGE

Joe Corbett, who gave some great displays during his stay in this country, has departed for Australia and Manila.

"Dropkick" Dan O'Connor is another wrestler to pass on. He returned to America on the "Mariposa."

Both these men expressed their appreciation of the kindness of the people of this country and both were high in their praise as to the way wrestling is governed in the Dominion. On behalf of fans we wish them the best of luck back under "Old Glory."

GEORGE COURTS
KARANGAHAPE ROAD

"FOR QUALITY GOODS AT LOWER PRICES"

George Court's Guinea Fur Felt Hat

Smart shape and all the new shades of grey, blue-grey, green, brown, navy, etc. Excellent quality hat.

Tweed Overcoats

Mostly in the popular double-breasted style. Our vast range provides for every taste and every pocket. From 35/6 to £7/10/-.

GEORGE COURT & SONS LTD.

Published by Consolidated Press of New Zealand, Chancery Chambers, Auckland, C.1.
and printed by Farrell Printing Co., Ltd.

By the 1941 season Lofty had been sent home from Egypt as his legs were not standing up to the hot Egyptian sun. He needed treatment for his varicose veins which had long been giving him trouble throughout his career. He was later able to resume wrestling as Sergeant-Major Lofty Blomfield, but on a smaller scale, and had many matches with Ken Kenneth, who was fast developing as a wrestler of great promise. Ken had been turned down for war service and told me one leg was shorter than the other, so he did home guard duties. I have found a record of Lofty and Ken meeting at least a dozen times in the 40s, mainly in Auckland, with one match on the North Shore in Birkenhead. Ken had some matches in Sydney's Leichhardt Stadium in 1941, where he was billed as Art Schischka. Lofty also had the odd match across the Tasman in the war years.

In 1942 no imported wrestlers were seen except for the odd American serviceman who called in. Wes Crowther and Charlie Walker from the U.S. Navy and Carr Gates another American serviceman, both proved very popular here. They had bouts with Frank Boric, Babe Wright, Charlie Ding (a European boy who settled on Waiheke Island and was also billed as "Iron Man" McGinty) Bill McIvor, and Jack Sissons.

Charlie Walker (American Serviceman) outside Auckland Town Hall in 1943.

1943 saw some of the U.S. servicemen still here and keen for some mat action, and it was all held in Auckland. Wes Crowther and Carr Gates had by now become big favorites, and the Auckland Town Hall was always full on a Monday evening. Lofty and Ken Kenneth were still doing well and had a series of matches against each other.

By 1944 Auckland, Wellington, Napier and Hastings were having wrestling contests, with some lesser known boys doing very well. Oscar Brock from Napier was one of them. Clem Shannon, Jack Prestney, Don Marsh, Bert Monastra, Harry Andrews, Bill Cook, Frank Boric, Arthur Reed, Tai Yates, Lofty and Ken Kenneth were still pulling in the crowds.

Jack Prestney (New Zealand) former national amateur champion.

Oscar Brock (above right) from Napier kept the sport alive and thriving around the Hawkes Bay area during the war years.

Wes Crowther (L) and Jack McLean (R) circa 1943. Crowther (a US serviceman from Salt Lake City, Utah) called in to Auckland for a few bouts at the Town Hall. McLean, a long-time professional referee and prominent Auckland hotelier, was involved in the sport for many years.

Wrestling contests were few and far between in 1945 with the majority of bouts being in Napier, and some middle weights and welterweights were having Championship contests.

With the war over, wrestling returned in a big way in 1946, with some top overseas boys coming in for the first time. A team of 13 consisting of Earl McCready, Lofty Blomfield, Jack Claybourne, Ken Kenneth, Lou Newman, King Elliott, John Katan, Hank Kaempfer, Harry Andrews, Babe Small, George Pencheff, Herb Meller and Fred Atkins made the wrestling-hungry fans extremely happy with their many bouts across the country.

For me personally, 1946 was a big year, as I was allowed to go to my first wrestling match for my 13th birthday. It was in Hastings and I was very excited to watch Earl McCready and George Pencheff go for eight rounds. I was hooked on the sport after that, and it was to play a big part in my life, along with my other favourite sport of boxing.

I started making scrapbooks of pictures of wrestlers and boxers in 1946, and am still doing the same today, some seventy years later. Some would say I never grew up, but today's fans don't realise just how huge the sport was here. If you asked kids at school who the Prime Minister of New Zealand was, not many would know, but if you asked who Earl McCready or Lofty Blomfield was you would get a huge response. Living in smaller towns I only got to see live wrestling and boxing matches three or four times a year. But I was glued to my radio every other night of the week for news of my mat heroes.

African American Jack Claybourne was one my favourites during that time and was one of the finest athletes to ever step inside the roped arena. Known as "Jumping" Jack and "The Black Shadow", Jack collected more money and fame than any other African American ring athlete since the heyday of Joe Louis.

The colourful American with the beaming smile was well known in New Zealand and Australia and set attendance records wherever he appeared. Jack was born and raised in the Missouri countryside and led the normal, healthy life of a farmer's son. As a lad, Jack kept company with a bunch of youngsters interested in the boxing game. He frequently worked out with them. Asked to substitute for an injured mate one night, the young hopeful had his first attempt at ring fame as a light-heavyweight boxer. After winning easily, Jack decided that here was the life, and began boxing in preliminaries around the fight clubs.

Wrestling, however, attracted him before he had proceeded much further in the boxing game. Its foremost feature in Jack's book, were the extra years it enabled one to remain an active athlete. So wrestling it was, and Jack claimed that at 16, he was the world's youngest professional wrestler.

Late in 1935, the young Negro defeated Stacy Hall in a prelim bout in Kansas City. He dropkicked Hall out of action in double-quick time.

Claybourne had closely watched the great Notre Dame footballer "Jumping" Joe Savoldi, and decided he could kick higher. After years of trying and many bone-jarring falls, Jack's kick reached the spectacular height of six and a half feet

American wrestler Jack Claybourne looking as sharp and as stylish as ever.

Claybourne's first main event was against Gus Karras, again at Kansas City, with Jack winning the best of three falls. There was no lack of activity for him after this success and engagements followed in many cities, black wrestlers being then still a novelty. Jack returned home to his birthplace of Boston to figure in a "local interest" bout against Bobby Stuart. World heavyweight boxing champion, Joe Louis, was referee. Jack was again top man.

Jack was the claimant of the World Coloured Heavyweight Championship, which he said he won from Rufus Jones in 1943. Such titles, of course are similar to "World Jewish Championship" and world "Junior" crowns, purely the figments of enterprising promoter's imaginations. There are dozens of them, with numerous claimants for each.

But at the same time, few African American wrestlers reached the heights that Jack Claybourne did.

It was 1946 when Jack first set foot in New Zealand and he wrestled 26 bouts. His two drawn matches with the Canadian Earl McCready were outstanding. He defeated New Zealand Champion Lofty Blomfield along with Ken Kenneth, Lou Newman and Harry Andrews.

In Australia he caused a sensation when he vaulted over the referee's head with a flying dropkick and landed flush on the button of Tiger Jogindar Singh to gain a fall. The Australian's loved Jack, and he had several hundred contests there, tangling with "Dirty" Dick Raines, Chief Little Wolf, LaVerne Baxter, Bob Wagner, Jessie James, Leo Jensen, Dutch Hefner, Al Costello, "Killer" Karl Davis, Emil Koroschenko, Arjan Das, Dean Detton, Frank Valois, and countless other top-liners.

In his New Zealand contests Jack managed to break even with Lofty Blomfield but, as many before him had done, found Earl McCready too tough, losing several times to the Empire titleholder. But Jack was one of those fortunate athletes--there are not many of them--who pack the crowds in regardless of whether he won or lost. In 1949 he became a top figure in the mat sport in Hawaii, where he wrestled under the banner of the former Russian Al Karasick, an early New Zealand favourite. There he won the Hawaiian "Junior" Heavyweight title, which is apparently up for competition among wrestlers of under the sixteen stone mark. He lost the championship to Bobby Managoff ten months later.

Jack had a great regard for lucky charms. He could be seen entering the ring with a small silver object suspended from around his neck. It was an English austerity threepence sent to him from Cairo by a woman tourist who had seen him wrestle in New Zealand.

Jack was the first African American to wrestle professionaly in New Zealand. He arrived here unknown and left as one of the greatest draw cards in New Zealand wrestling history. Other black stars to appear here have been "Bearcat" Wright, Don Kindred, Luther Lindsay, and Ricky Waldo, but none of them enjoyed the popularity of "Jumping" Jack.

Perhaps Jack's best opponent in New Zealand was the Bulgarian-Australian, George Pencheff. These two were of a similar weight and both agile and clever aerial specialists. One Wellington match is still remembered by the fans there. Wrestling matches have come and gone without even rippling the surface of public scepticism, but the Claybourne - Pencheff battle in Wellington provoked a wave of enthusiasm among the capital city's mat fans that will take a long time to subside. So spectacular was the bout that a noted wrestling writer said he never hoped to witness a better match. Highlight of the bout - and for that matter, highlight of the wrestling season - came in the final round. Claybourne had dropkicked Pencheff - Pencheff had dropkicked Claybourne. Then the crowd came to its feet with a mighty roar as both men left the mat at the same time and collided feet- first in mid air with two of the most sensationally executed dropkicks ever seen in the Wellington Town Hall. To the reporters and other ringsiders it looked as if the two men were flying about six feet off the mat when they collided. The impact of course rocked them both. Claybourne was the first to stagger to his feet, but before he could gather his faculties, Pencheff had sprung from the mat like a panther to land another dropkick. The crowd was in a frenzy, and when Claybourne let fly with yet another dropkick, the spectators nearly brought the roof down.

I had the pleasure of meeting Jack on a few occasions when I was an amateur wrestler. The dressing rooms were all close together and we got to talk to all the top world wrestlers that came here.

A gentleman in and out of the ring, the late Jack Claybourne will always be remembered as a true sportsman. Jack committed suicide many years ago now. In advancing years Jack was getting less bookings and, as he had only ever known wrestling, he probably felt he had nothing left to live for.

The author with Jack Claybourne at the Wanganui Opera House in 1951. Also in the photo (top) is a local amateur wrestler called Bernie Dunstan.

1947 saw the return of the perennials Earl McCready and Lofty Blomfield. Paul Boesch returned after an outstanding war record in the U.S. Army, in which he was highly decorated for bravery. Many of the boys not only took risks in the ring, but were heroes in the war as well. Paul Boesch had previously been here in 1936 and 1939 and was a huge favourite. He was well educated and a great speaker; when not wrestling he often helped with the radio broadcasts, which were hugely popular.

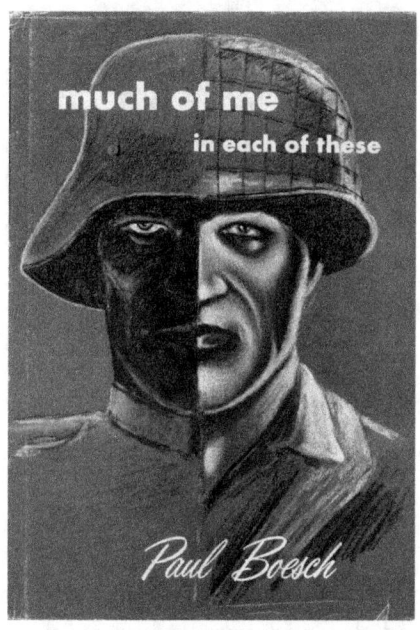

Above: The front cover of one of Paul Boesch's many books; this one a book of poetry. Paul wrote one of the poems, 'Hour Glass' whilst visiting Taumuranui during a wrestling tour in 1939. Over the years Paul always sent me copies of his work and many photographs. He last came out for a visit in 1984 whilst acting as the guest MC for a large wrestling tournament and we spent some time together revisiting the glory years. The first thing Paul did on his arrival in New Zealand was to take his second wife to his favourite location - Rotorua - a place he fell in love with on his previous visits.

Newcomers in 1947 were Jim Henry, Jim Wright, Otto Kuss, Tom Rice, Kay Bell and Tommy O'Toole. It proved to be another great season with the fans packing out the halls all over the country.

Jim Wright puts an "arm-bar" on Otto Kuss: Wanganui Opera house (1947).

In 1948 a couple of leading American boys came here in Joe Pazandak and Len "Butch" Levy. These boys had class and were known as "shooters" back in the States. In other words they could wrestle, and pin the best wrestlers around. These two had excellent matches with Earl McCready and our own Lofty Blomfield. Pat Fraley, Dutch Hefner, Marvin Jones, Bill Kuusisto and Eddie Scarfe (who was from Australia) made up the 1948 team.

Ken Kenneth and Bill Kuusisto figured in a match in Auckland which proved to be Bill Kuusisto's last ever wrestling match. Bill had more matches in New Zealand in 1948 than any other wrestler, and he will always remember New Zealand as the place where his wrestling career came to an abrupt end.

(Clockwise) Tommy O'Toole, Tom Rice, Jim Wright and Kay Bell (bottom left). Kay Bell also had some work in the movie 'Samson and Delilah' as a stand-in for Victor Mature.

Ken had applied a back-loop slam, and somehow Bill had broken a rib, which had punctured his lung. Although wrestlers knew how to fall there was always the odd exception where you could fall badly. It was an accident Ken Kenneth never forgot and it played on his mind for many months as to whether to give up his chosen career or not.

Bill Kuusisto ended up in Auckland hospital in a serious condition. His excellent physical condition enabled him to pull through, but his wrestling career was finished and he went on to become one of America's most respected wrestling referees. Every time Ken Kenneth went to the United States his first call was to visit his old opponent, as the two had by now become great friends.

Bill Kuusisto (left) in his prime and (below) with Ken Kenneth who is pointing to the offending injury which put Bill out of active competition. Every time Ken Kenneth went to the USA his first port of call was to visit his former rival. Ken aways felt bad about retiring Bill prematurely. Kuusisto stayed in the game and went on to become a prominent referee.

Bill Kuusisto referees a bout between Dick Raines and Abe Kashey in the United States. Raines is about to win the match with his famous 'Back-Breaker' move.

1949 brought some outstanding talent in Eric "The Chest" Holmback, (later to become a huge talent in world wrestling as Yukon Eric), Pat Fraley, (The Singing Cowboy), Ray Gunkel, Tiger Joginder, Len Levy, Pete Managoff, Dick Raines, Pierre LaSalle, Johnny Sepeda, Tommy O'Toole, and the old faithfulls Lofty Blomfield, Ken Kenneth and Earl McCready. Ray Gunkel wasn't too impressive here and was sent packing - he later became a wrestling superstar in the USA.

Sadly for New Zealand fans this was to be Lofty Blomfield's last year of ring action. This much loved and respected New Zealander was having more trouble with his legs, so wisely decided to pack the game in and become manager of the Whangarei Hotel. Lofty's name was a household one for almost twenty years and it was sad to see him go. However he continued to keep in the limelight with his charity work and the Intellectually Handicapped Children was his favourite. He gave untold time to his favourite charities and did tremendous work for them.

In 1938 when the late Prime Minister, Michael Joseph Savage was recuperating from a serious illness he was asked how he felt. "I'm getting along fine" he said, "I'll soon be able to take a fall out of Lofty Blomfield."

It was no secret that the "big match" of 1949 would have brought Lofty and Ken Kenneth together in a New Zealand title match. Ken and Lofty had met on more than twenty previous occasions. Ken's improvement suggested that an outdoor attendance of 30,000 was a huge possibility. However, it was not to be and Ken took over as New Zealand Heavyweight Champion.

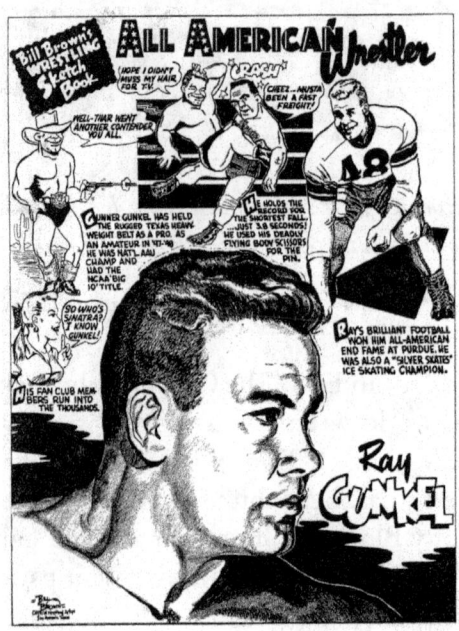

Above (left) a promotional postcard for American wrestler Ray Gunkel and (above right) Pete Managoff. Gunkel only had one match in New Zealand and didn't go over too well. The Texan went on to much wider fame and popularity in his home country, winning several titles along the way. This photo of Managoff was taken in Gisborne by a school friend of mine. I managed to get it signed later the same year.

A HISTORY OF WRESTLING IN NEW ZEALAND

Clockwise (from top left); Tiger Joginder, Len Levy, "The Singing Cowboy" Pat Fraley (with guitar), Johnny Sepeda. All of the above had a number of bouts across New Zealand at the end of the 1940s.

Joe Pazandak of Minneapolis, Minnesota.

One of the most accomplished wrestlers ever to come to New Zealand, Joe Pazandak also did a great deal to encourage amateur wrestling in this country. One night in the 1950s I popped my head around Joe's dressing-room door prior to the wrestling, but he was deep in conversation with Pat O'Connor's dad (Pat went on to become New Zealand's only world wrestling champion). Earlier that same day I had seen Pazandak getting into Pat's dad's pick-up truck and he appeared to take up the whole of the back of the truck - he looked massive across the shoulders.

Wrestling took place on a Thursday night in the capital. Above is a typical programme from the regular events at the Town Hall.

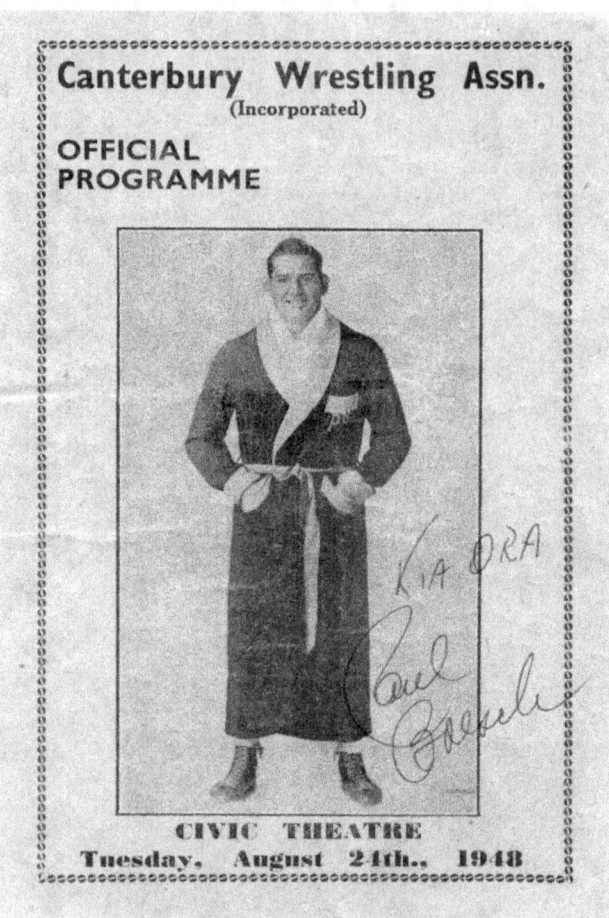

Tuesday was the night for wrestling in Christchurch; usually booked for several months of the year between April and October. All the top names would appear all over the country thanks to Walter Miller's efforts.

A HISTORY OF WRESTLING IN NEW ZEALAND

Another Christchurch programme - this event featured the popular Canadian Earl McCready going up against "Dirty" Dick Raines from Texas. The Kiwi fans were very knowledgeable and the promoters were able to put the international stars on to packed houses. Lofty Blomfield was very popular, but it didn't take a New Zealand wrestler to sell the place out. Even with around six amateurs on the cards wrestling nights were popular from Invercargill in the south to Kaikohe in the far north.

Fred Atkins was born in 1910 in Westport, New Zealand, but was claimed by the Australians to have been born in Bundaburg, Queensland. He was a very tough character and had some great matches with Chief Little Wolf all over Australia. He eventually settled in Canada - his real name was Atkinson.

George Pencheff wrestled all the greats, including Jim Londos the world champion. He was a great aerial wrestler with excellent drop-kicks. He wrestled throughout the 1930s - 40s and 50s. He was one of the first wrestlers I saw in action live when he wrestled Earl McCready at the Municipal Theatre in Hastings, New Zealand.

Marvin Jones came from Texas in the USA and in the 1940s he teamed with another 'bad man' of the ring Hans Schnabel - winning many bouts in and around his home state. In the 1950s Marvin became a prominent referee in the States along with Paul Boesch and Dick Raines. He was very popular in New Zealand and had wins over Lofty Blomfield, Jack Claybourne and Bill Kuusisto.

A HISTORY OF WRESTLING IN NEW ZEALAND

Herb Meller was born in New York City in 1908 - the son of German immigrants. He wore long black leggings to cover up the effects of childhood polio. Better known in America as Hans Schnabel, he wrestled in a champion tag-team with his brother Fritz. Schnabel was their mother's maiden name. Herb's daughter confirmed his actual name was Herbert Moeller.

With the Compliments of
LEO DEMETRAL

Leo Demetral was known as the "Wrestling Globetrotter". Well-known in Australia and England, Leo appeared in New Zealand in 1948. He lived in South Africa for a time and worked as a physical education instructor on the Union Castle ships. Born in Greece in 1913 his real name was Stathis Nicolaou.

Big Jim Henry had 27 matches in New Zealand in 1948, but picked up a bad head cold and was released early from his contract (they would usually have about 40 matches). He beat Lofty Blomfield in two out of five matches. He was known in America as Jim "Goon" Henry and under a mask as "The Green Hornet".

Dutch Hefner was a big name in Australia where he fitted right into the rougher style of wrestling. He wrestled under various masks in America and had about 20 bouts in New Zealand - beating Joe Pazandak and Lofty Blomfield - so he was pretty good.

John Katan (born in Ukraine in 1901) he was raised in Alberta, Canada from the age of four. He was known to all as "Honest John". He never lost a single match in a three-year amateur career and as a professional in 1940, beat Earl McCready to win the British Empire Crown. He was well-known in Australia where he was a frequent visitor.

Lou Newman was known as Lou "Shoulder" Newman for obvious reasons. Born in Canada in 1913 his real name was Reino Nyman. He wrestled all the greats during his career and was holder of the World Tag-Team title with Hans Schnable (1955-57). Lou was known as a globe-trotter and wrestled around the world from Honolulu to New Zealand, USA, South Africa, Australia, Japan and Mexico. He also won the Canadian Heavyweight belt from Albet Mills in 1955 in Edmonton, Canada.

Eric "The Chest" Holmback

Little did we know in 1949 when watching wrestling import Eric Holmback, that we would be watching a future superstar of world wrestling. Some years later he became known as "Yukon Eric". He became a huge star at New York's Madison Square Garden and Toronto's Maple Leaf Gardens.

Eric arrived here an unknown in 1949, but soon impressed with his ruggedness and a will to win at all costs. The big Alaskan from Fairbanks in the frozen north had some sterling tussles here against some of the top names in world wrestling. He recorded wins over two of our greatest ever visitors; Len "Butch" Levy and the great Canadian Earl McCready. He was a tremendous draw card, and his matches with our own Lofty Blomfield and Ken Kenneth had the "House Full" signs out in quick time.

His New Zealand season came to an abrupt end after only twenty-one bouts when he faced "Cowboy" Pat Fraley in Hastings. The big man left New Zealand with his jaw wired together, while subsisting on milk sucked through a straw. His jaw was broken in several places after getting in the way of an elbow jolt.

The 'New Zealand Sporting Life & Referee' had the following to say about Eric;

"Eric "The Chest" Holmback, the wrestler with the fifty-seven and a half inch chest, came to New Zealand with little publicity, but after he had played rough with Lofty Blomfield and put him out of action he developed into a great draw card."

DAVE CAMERON

Eric "The Chest" Holmback (above) in a classic studio pose and (left) with his two huskies whilst outdoor training in the snowy wilds of Alaska.

When Eric arrived in New Zealand Wallie Ingram wrote the following in the Southern Cross newspaper.

"ERIC "THE CHEST" HOLMBACK PRODUCT OF LUMBER CAMP.

Soon after leaving San Francisco by air for New Zealand, American wrestler Eric Holmback met the patron of the Dominion of New Zealand Wrestling Union, travelling on the same aircraft on his return from an important conference in London. But Eric Holmback, who wrestles Len Levy in Wellington on Thursday night, was not aware he had met the Patron until the big wrestler walked into the Wellington Union's office in Wellington yesterday. He knew he had met Mr. Peter Fraser, Prime Minister of New Zealand, and had had conversation with him, but he did not know that Mr. Fraser was also patron of the wrestling concern for which he will be wrestling:

"They call Holmback "The Chest" in New York, and for good reason, too. Holmback is twenty-six inches across the shoulders. Big, rugged and tough, Holmback uses a style that is generally classed as a lumberjack style among grapplers themselves, and the barrelchested half Eskimo never hesitates to use the foot whenever the opportunity presents itself.

Holmback's tremendous strength is one of his biggest assets. Before he knew what a weight was in the gymnasium he bested all the other kids in the lumber camp where his father worked, at tests of strength that included lifting logs and huge stones. One of their favourite pastimes was trying to tear young trees out of the ground, and it was always young Eric who could tear the thickest and oldest tree out with the least trouble.

Weighing eighteen stone eight pounds this blond Alaskan stands six foot one inch and should be a sensation. He is not a flying tackler - he reckons he'd wreck too many ring ropes by propelling his bulk against them but he has a backbreaker which he modestly claims is more efficient than that used by Dick Raines.

Raines uses his speciality hold by holding his opponent aloft and dropping him over the knee. Holmback drops them on his shoulder to give them a solid bump before he slams them to the mat.

Wrestling in New York on Monday May 2nd, Holmback took an aircraft to San Francisco on Tuesday and arrived in New Zealand on Saturday. He was keen to get working out in a gymnasium once he arrived in New Zealand and it would seem that, like Pazandak and Levy, Holmback will spend a lot of his spare time - if he gets any - working out in the various gymnasiums.

Len Levy, who will be conceding approximately one stone in weight to Holmback when they meet at the Wellington Town Hall on Thursday night, is one of the fastest of the big men and, against the rugged tactics of Holmback "I like an opponent who will come in and make things willing," says Holmback "there should be something doing all the time". Incidentally, the preferential bookings for this match they opened yesterday are a record for any match in the last two seasons, and if Holmback satisfies the Wellington wrestling fans as he did those in New York he should not regret his visit to New Zealand."

Eric Holmback did manage to beat the highly rated Len Levy in that Wellington match, and the following week was matched against the rough, tough "Dirty" Dick Raines. The Wellington paper recorded the following.

RAINES LOSES TO HOLMBACK IN THRILLING CONTEST.

"Dick Raines (17. 6.) the Texas toughman, was cheered as he climbed into the Wellington Town Hall ring last night to meet the big-chested Alaskan Eric Holmback (18 stone, 12 pounds), and this rather novel experience nonplussed him. After generally having the better of a rugged, but scientific match - one of the most thrilling of the season - Raines took a fall in the third round, but was badly shaken by a series of slams in the sixth round and unable to continue though he did try after the decision had been given to Holmback."

Ken Kenneth, who became firm friends with Eric in New Zealand, later met up with him in Canada, and tells many stories about the incredible toughness of the man. Ken told me that promoter Jack Tunney used to parade Eric around the streets of Toronto in an open-topped Cadillac as publicity for his forthcoming matches. "Yukon" Eric as he was now known, was wearing only a bush shirt with short sleeves, open at the chest, the temperature was way below zero.

Ken also told me of his immense strength. "He was as strong as a horse. He looked as though a train couldn't knock him down."
There was the time Eric had his eye on a new Pontiac Convertible. He walked into the car sales yard in his big knee boots and the salesman ignored him. "How much is this one?" he asked another salesman. "Thirty five hundred dollars," said the man. "I'll take it," said Eric. He walked over to a table and emptied the paper bag he was carrying. It was filled with money. "Take it out of this," he told the startled salesman.

Eric sent this signed photo to me in 1949. Requests for autographs and photos went through the Dominion Union and came back via the post with a two-penny stamp.

Then of course, there was the historic match in Montreal, where Eric was wrestling "Killer" Kowalski, who was then at his peak. Kowalski jumped at Eric off the top rope with a knee drop. Eric's ear was torn clean off. It left only the lobe on the left side. (Eric's ears were slightly cauliflowered, heavy with scar tissue, which made such an occurrence possible.) The referee bent down and picked the ear up off the floor.

The crowd were shouting "Fake. Fake. Fake." but Eric stood there bleeding all over the place. Eric and the ear were rushed to hospital, but it was too late. They were unable to sew it back on.

The legendary Wladek or Walter "Killer" Kowalski.

Eric was very much a loner. He met a girl from Weston and they were married in Georgia while travelling on the road. She was a pretty girl and they had children. One day Eric walked into the wrestling office and asked Jack Tunney for his wages. He said he was heading for Florida. Eric hopped into his big convertible and headed south but he didn't go to Florida. He drove to the small town of Georgia where he and his wife had been married.

He was at the peak of his popularity at this stage and was a very wealthy man. Big Eric drove his Lincoln Continental into the churchyard at the little church where he had been married and parked it. He wrote a note to his sister in Iowa, and then took out his gun and shot himself. We will never know what caused Eric to be so depressed, but it was a sad end for the remarkable wrestler.

The Lofty Blomfield Story

The following 15 or so pages are straight out of the mouth of the man himself. In the late 1960s Lofty and I were working on a book for Whitcombe and Tombs (nowadays known as Whitcoulls). Their publishing department was located in Christchurch and they were very keen on publishing what would have been one of the first New Zealand sports biographies - long before the masses of rugby biographies you see on the shelves now.

The idea fizzled out after I returned to the U.K. for a year and by the time I returned to New Zealand Lofty had little to no interest as he had his hands full operating his hotel in Whangerei and was heavily involved in the Intellectually Handicapped Children's (IHC) charity.

The piece by Lofty is a mine of information and I always had hopes of publishing it someday in book form.

My first ambition was to be a jockey. I used to get up at the crack of dawn and creep out from my home in Takapuna to go along to Alison's racing stables for a gallop along the beach on one of the many good horses that used to be trained there. I cultivated the correct riding attitude with my knees hunched up and pictured myself riding the winners of the big races at Ellerslie and returning in triumph to the birdcage with the roar of the multitude in my ears.

But the roar I hear nowadays is a different kind of roar - the loud cries of the wrestling fans almost lifting the roof off with their shouts of encouragement and hoots of disdain. At one time I used to take these hoots seriously. A mild "boo" cut me to the quick. A chorus of them made me feel like a social outcast. Nowadays the "boos" don't worry me. In fact I don't care two hoots;

For the crowd that hoots will often come back again to hoot some more. And that is all good from the professional wrestler's point of view. Besides I am not entirely friendless. My admirers are most embarrassing sometimes in their expressions. For instance, one night after a bout in Wanganui a man came to my dressing-room asking for an autograph. There was nothing new about this. Autograph hunters, like trachoma, or "eye-blight" are in some ways the wrestlers curse, though, of course, it is always a pleasure to oblige a sincere admirer. However, this gentleman was something new among autograph hunters, for instead of the usual autograph book or piece of paper, he had a pair of lady's silk "scanties" and he wanted me to autograph these. It is always a pleasure to oblige a lady, and I duly "signed on the dotted line." However, I suggested to the gentleman that in future, before bringing his girl friend to the wrestling, he should provide her with an autograph book.

One day in Marton there was a primary school rugby tournament on and about 75 boys were in the street when I came along. One of them produced his autograph book and bailed me up. None of the others had autograph books but one of them was resourceful and ducked into a shop to return with a 3d. Notebook and a pencil. In this I wrote my signature. After that all the other boys went into the shop and completely denuded it of notebooks, while I stood on the pavement, signing left and right.

Another novel experience was in Sydney where I had torn off the sole of Alec Lundyn's wrestling shoe in a match with him. The sole was half off and the nails were sticking into me, so I pulled it right off and tossed it out of the ring. Someone took it as a souvenir and a day or two later came along and asked me to autograph it, which I duly did.

Once in the train, coming up from Wellington, a man came to me and asked me to autograph his copy of 'Truth'. I did. In this case truth was stranger than fiction. People seem to value a wrestler's signature even if it is only scrawled across a cigarette packet, or on the back of an envelope. I have even been asked to autograph a piece of referee's shirt which had been torn during a struggle in the ring.

One of the most remarkable evidences of the popularity of wrestling is the number of people who write to the wrestlers, and my own 'fan mail' has reached astonishing proportions. People send letters to my private address in Auckland, to various hotels I stop at, to the Wrestling Associations, and care of my relatives. Every day scores of letters arrive, and sometimes they run into hundreds. It is a real man-sized job attending to them.

Most of these letters are couched in flattering terms, but some are definitely hostile. One man, signing himself "Kruse-ite," said if I had the guts to meet Kruse I would be carried out feet first. I did meet him, and retained consciousness throughout, but he beat me on points.

Another man who could scarcely be called a Blomfield fan, had cut out an advertisement for my match with Danny Dusek. It read "Lofty Blomfield v Danny Dusek." But after the Lofty Blomfield he had written "and Charlie Pollard." (Charlie Pollard was the Auckland referee at that time.) Very neat.

This is the sort of brickbat that is sometimes tucked away among the bouquets: *"You are the world's lowest and worst wrestler. You are just an elbow jolter and octopus clamp artist and you can't even do the octopus clamp properly because you have to get the referee to undo it."* I need scarcely point out that in more impartial circles it is considered the wrestler's duty only to apply the grips, and let someone else worry about getting them unstuck.

One member of the anti-Blomfield brigade predicted disaster for me when I met Woods. According to him, I would be just a bit of rag with which Woods would wipe the floor. I would be tied in knots, torn to pieces and ground to powder. Fortunately I escaped this deplorable fate. I had two matches with Woods, winning one and drawing the other.

The people who write to me range from children who can't spell to old men of 70 and over - some of whom still can't spell. There are people from far away in the back blocks, people from the cities, people from the far south and far north, all close followers of wrestling through the medium of radio, even if they have never seen a match. I will give you a selection of these letters, just culled at random from a recent day's mail, and I hope readers get as much fun out of them as I did. Here is one from a keen wrestling fan who lives in Russell St. Feilding:

"Mr Bloomfield, Dear Lofty, Thank you very much for the thrilling evening you gave us on Saturday last, especially my husband, who, as he works at nights rarely hears a wrestling bout but he is very keen on the "local boy". When we heard you speak from 1ZM my husband said: "I like Lofty all the more now as I think his voice shows personality," at which we all got in a few remarks about elbow jolts just to see him hit the roof, which he did and said he would write then and there to you backing you up. Our family are all boys so if you could possibly spare us a photo of yourself our household would be treading on air. I might add that when any of your bouts are broadcast I have to recite all the details over again at 4.30a.m. for my husband, and I'm feeling pretty good. I can even show how to put on an octopus clamp."

I certainly got a great kick out of this letter, for I like to think of the good lady in Feilding clapping an octopus clamp on the family breadwinner when he comes home after a night's toil. All I hope is that she can get it undone properly and does not have to send an S.O.S. to the next-door neighbour.

Here is a good effort from a resident of Titoki St., Penrose.

"Mr Lofty Bloomfield (sic)

Dear Sir,
Being keen wrestle fan and having see you in action so often and also listening to Mr Hutter speaking of you I have summoned up enough courage to meet you but only for your photo that will be the only win I hope to get from you even then you can get the clamp on at any stage of it. You know Lofty to be fair to you fellows I would suggest radio of matches be cut out. From what I can gather they go a few times have good look at holds and then listen in. You would I feel sure get bigger house. I will close Lofty, good luck. While I am writing you as regards eyes. I do not know what wrong with your eyes but seems the same if sweat run into them they get blood streaks and sight gets blurred. Eye specialists say otaprine (?) drops three times day but I kept some drops and find after 20 years they were no good they lose strength in few weeks but fellow said to use bluestone four pounds. I found few drops bluestone water also works wonders. If using just make water light blue. It never hurts good eyes but stings bad ones. Anyway Lofty I close again it's good pen I got and can't stop writing so excuse scribble."

The reference to eye trouble is of course to the trachoma or eye blight which bothers wrestlers, though it is not nearly as bad in N.Z. as in America. Believe me, anyone who has had one experience of it doesn't want any more. The treatment for it is about the most painful thing I know.

The same gentleman who sent me the prescription for eye trouble also sent me a patent grip of his own devising which he urged me to copyright. Unluckily there is no copyright over wrestling grips and in any case I am afraid the directions given were a little puzzling. As my correspondent remarked, "It seems all right on paper." They generally do.

A Tuakau fan sends some advise:

"Dear Lofty, I am writing to ask you for a photo of yourself. Could you tell me if you train Ken Kenneth. Hoping you beat old Kruse and have every success.

P.S. --- Look out for that hammerlock as he held Boesch for six minutes"

A Herekino listener notes a family talent:

"I have never seen you in the flesh but I knew your brother Trevor by sight. He used to play for the Northcote A's (juniors) in '31 while I played for the B's. I was going to St. Peter's College there at the time and if you are as good in the ring with headlocks as he was on the field with them well I guess you are another "Strangler" Lewis in the bud."

I was very keen on rugby myself and it was my greatest ambition to get into the All Blacks, but I never got beyond provincial football. My brother is playing for the Takapuna Senior B team this season.
Now for the ladies. This is from a Hamilton girl:

"Mr. Blomfield, there is one thing I would really like you to do and that is to beat Bob Kruse. I saw in the Sporting Life that he was bragging but I feel sure that you could beat him. I have bet for you with a friend so if he beats you I will lose five shillings - Dorothy B."

Too bad Dorothy, that Kruse beat me on points. Suppose we blame the referee.

From a girl at Newstead, Hamilton:

"All the members of our household are ardent admirers of yours and think you are a wonderful wrestler, a splendid sport, and a first class elbow-jolter, so as a souvenir we would love to have one of your photographs. We have seen you wrestle in Hamilton and are now eagerly awaiting your return, so that we shall be able to witness another of your thrilling matches."

This is the sort of letter that warms the cockles of the old heart and makes one feel as if being a professional wrestler is the most marvelous job in the world. But here is one, also from a lady, which is like a douche of cold water.

"To Mr. L Blomfield. Sir: You are the dirtiest exponent of a dirty game. They shouldn't allow you in the ring, let alone on the air. I always send my children to bed when wrestling is being broadcast. (Mrs.) Laura S----, Opotiki."

But it shouldn't really be necessary to send the children to bed, Mrs. S---- Why not just switch them onto another station and listen to the chamber music. Or do you like listening in to the "dirty game" yourself?

The following from a girl at Bridge Street, Bulls, is a real masterpiece.

"Dear Mr. Blomfield, I have been admiring you for some time so at least I thought I thought I'd write. It's grand to have a great New Zealand wrestler in our country who has a good chance of beating Macready. I listen to your bouts with extreme interest, and it's good when you're wrestling, because we always get some fireworks, and that's what we're wanting these days. I agree with what Jack Forsgren says about you. He says you can dish it out and take it too. That's what I like about you. You let the other fellow give you what for, and don't run away like some of the other wrestlers.

I think your octopus clamp is a great affair. I thought you had got Macready caught in it about a month ago and I was sorry he managed to pull round.

Could you please answer this letter personally. You can guess I would be pleased if you could. I am enclosing a confession slip which I hope you will fill in. It's nice to have some facts about your favourite wrestler.

Wishing you every success here and in other countries,
Yours sincerely,
      Merle H------."

Merle's "confessional slip" is a remarkable document. I give some of the questions, with my answers:

"What is your favourite name?"
Why, Merle, of course.

"Who is your favourite film star?"
How about Baby Le Roy?

"Who is your favourite radio star?"
This one is easy - Gordon Hutter.

"Which type of holiday do you like most?"
Any type of holiday does me.

"What is your favourite flower?"
I can't say I'm up on flowers, but I like cauliflowers - when someone else is wearing them:

"What is your favourite hobby?"
Sleeping.

"What is your favourite colour?"
Red, except when my opponent is seeing it.

"What would you most like to be?"
Rich.

"Who is your favourite author?"
The reporter who gave me my last good write-up.

"Which season of the year do you prefer?"
Speaking generally, the festive season.

"What is your pet aversion?"
My opponent.

At the bottom of this questionnaire is a line which reads: *"This is the confession of.............."*
            But I don't think I had better sign it.

Here is a girl from Robin Street, Taihape who says:

"My mother backs Earl McCready while I am a real Blomfieldite, and stick up for you every time. If only you can get the clamp on well and truly it will fix him and I will feel very proud of you then Lofty. I hope you don't mind me calling you Lofty, because I am that used to it that I have been writing it here.
I remain a Blomfieldite,
Rene W--------"

Another lady, Mrs. A. of Manning St. Newton, Auckland, addresses me respectfully as "Dear Mr. Blomfield" but I really think I prefer:

"Dear Lofty."
A proud father writes from away south at Waitaki to ask me for a photograph for his six year old son who *"has a surprisingly good knowledge of the holds for a kid and like yourself he can dish out some good elbow jolts."*

Another good one is from a nine- year- old boy at Sunny Downs, Ohaupo, who asks: *"Have you a good photograph of yourself in your tites that you could give me please?"*

A personal request from Wharehuia, Stratford:

"I have a brother George up your way somewhere. He is a jockey and he lives with a Mr. Rodgers at Remuera and if you happen to know of him I would be very pleased if you would give him my address. I don't know the name of the street so I thought I would ask your assistance, as you know the surroundings up there."

Slightly ungrammatical note from Putaruru:

"I seen you wrestle only one to my regart (? Regret) and I wish I could see more of your matches. Can't you put a spoke in McCready's wheel?" A little boy from Kenyon Avenue, Mount Eden says, *"Please beat Bob Cruise. I am only ten."*

A Fencourt (Cambridge) admirer seeks a photograph, admitting that he is *"on the scrounge"*, and *"hoping you bowl all those other mugs out."* This might have sounded better had he left out the "other".
Some technical advise from Whangarei:

"As I am a New Zealand borne naturally one back up his country man. I would like to see you taking a won over McCready before he leaves here. If I were wrestling Mac I would go in whilst I was fresh and secure a fall and then keep on the defencive."

Another fan from Matamata advises me to *"put on my Rangitoto special every time."* It sounds like an ice-cream.

Well, there are hundreds more but I can't go on quoting forever. Many of these letters are funny and some a little pathetic, but they have this in common - their interest is not so much in Lofty Blomfield as in Lofty Blomfield the New Zealander.

Lofty (standing) in the process of putting Joe Savoldi to the mat (Wellington Town Hall 1936.)

MY FIRST TRIP TO THE STATES.

I landed in California on January 3, a Wednesday, and without any workout had my first match in a ten minute preliminary at Oakland, across the bay from San Francisco, on the following Saturday. My opponent was one Jim Healey, I beat him and got $35.00 but had an idea the performance did not impress the "heads" very much. Except for a friendly word in the right quarters from Dan Koloff, I had arrived in the U.S.A. unknown, and I had to make my own way.

I had another bout in Sacramento on the following Monday night and from then on began to get regular matches, until I got up to what are called main events. A wrestling programme there consists of usually five matches, two ten-minute preliminaries and a "Special," also of ten minutes and then a semifinal, of half an hour, followed by the main event, on which there is a two hour limit, two falls out of three to win.

The system of control and promoting is very efficient. In California there is a circuit of promoters, each in a different town. About a dozen in all, they have a central office at the St. Marks Hotel, Oakland, to which they contribute 5% of their gross takings, thus providing for upkeep of the office, which handles all the publicity as well as fixing up the matches. A promoter in say, Eureka, 300 miles north of San Francisco, will write down saying what wrestlers he would like. All other promoters do the same, and the central office does its best to meet the various requirements, though of course it cannot always do so. Every Monday a bulletin board is posted at the St. Marks Hotel showing the engagements of the various wrestlers for that week. Some wrestlers get only about one or two matches a week. After a while I began to get five and six matches a week. In fact one week I wrestled six matches and travelled 1,800 miles. This was my schedule (or "skedool" as the Americans would call it) for that week:

Monday night Wrestled in Oakland.
Tuesday night Wrestled in San Francisco and returned to Oakland.
Wednesday Flew to Los Angeles, 400 miles, wrestled there that night.
Thursday Flew back to Oakland, then motored to Santa Cruz to wrestle.
Friday drove to Fresno, 200 miles, wrestled there.
That night, back to Oakland after match.
Saturday Drove to Eureka, 300 miles north, wrestled there that night, back to Oakland after match reaching home 5a.m.Sunday.

That's pretty strenuous going, though of course travel in California is facilitated by the wonderful highway system and the splendid air services.

Compared with New Zealand one has to wrestle more often to make the same money. There is not enough money in it except for the "big shots", for matches to be "fixed", and I saw no evidence of this. If you fix a match you have to pay the loser. You can't do this if the winning end of the purse isn't pretty thick. Besides, the public like to see winners, not losers, so it wouldn't pay a man to run a stumer. The refereeing is good and police interference practically nil. Police have no jurisdiction once the men are in the ring. After that the wrestling commission has all the say. Referees let a lot go that would not be tolerated in New Zealand, but there as everywhere, the crowds like sportsmanship. I saw one referee who used to say "Come on, get in there, whaddya loafing for? If you don't get in I'll starp the match." Incidently, from the day I landed, Californians were exceedingly interested in my "curious accent," My friends used to introduce me to other people as a kind of special treat, so that they could hear me talk. More than one person asked me how I came to speak such good English. People were so fascinated by my "cute way of talking" that they would try and keep me talking and when I stopped would say: "Go on, talk some more."

Lofty becomes "Big Chief Many Moons Away" and an honourary member of the Cherokee nation.

The big shots in wrestling over there included Jim Browning, Savoldi, Wade, Detton (who is very popular) Hardy Kruskamp, and Chief Little Wolf. Little Wolf is a full-blooded Indian and a really good wrestler. Before I left I wrestled in world's championship elimination bouts in Los Angeles, and got to the final elimination round when I met Browning. after 20 minutes I was knocked out with an aeroplane spin. I wrestled six times in Los Angeles, it's a great city.

When I arrived the first thought of the promoting organisation was to pin a name on to me. They didn't like "Lofty" so they compromised with "Lufty". After much thought they picked "Basil" as a suitable surname for me, and under this horrible pseudonym I made all my appearances. So although I am Lofty Blomfield in New Zealand and Walter Browning in Australia, I am Lufty Basil in California.

They didn't bill me as "the New Zealand cave-man" or anything like that. Most of the wrestlers who use such titles have adopted them for themselves, though here and there the radio announcers or the press coin a suitable name, like that bestowed on Pinto, "The Chicago Bad Boy".

Half the wrestlers over there are what New Zealanders would call "dirty", the Cy Williams type. No one would take any notice of Williams over there. I went there as a nobody, thinking that better than to start with a flourish of trumpets which I mightn't be able to live up to. I just did my best and I think it paid. After a while the promoters started to notice their receipts got better when I was on the bill, and so I got more and more matches. Although it was hard work, I enjoyed every minute of it.

I found it was good tactics to start off by wrestling clean and let the other fellow start the rough stuff. The crowd would then get incensed and start booing him. After that one could, if so inclined, get away with murder. One learns a lot about human psychology when wrestling.
I did such a lot of travelling that I became quite an authority on Californian roads. Petrol is only 20 cents a gallon over there - 10d. in our money. It is the motorists' paradise. New cars are cheap, and second hand cars may be bought for a song. The lounges of the service stations are fitted up like hotel lounges. If you ask an attendant for "benzine" or "petrol" he says, "We don't stock that," quite seriously. Tell him you want gas, and he understands you. You don't buy just a gallon or two. You say "Fill her up." It will only cost you about a dollar.

The maximum speed on the highways is 45m.p.h. and less in the towns. Efficient highway patrolmen, armed with revolvers, keep check on speedsters. Summary jurisdiction is the rule. The offending motorist is hauled off immediately to a court and fined on the spot, a much better way than our system of waiting three weeks to get a summons for a trivial offence. Some towns there have a system of fining you a dollar a mile for every mile you go above the speed limit. Traffic on main roads has the right-of-way every time. There is no right hand rule. Coming out of a by-road a "boulevard stop sign" warns you to stop and look each way. After a while it becomes a habit. Right down to the less important roads, the traffic on secondary thoroughfares gives way. When you might be puzzled as to which street is the more important the boulevard stop sign helps you out.

The Californian climate is very mild down round Los Angeles, but I found San Francisco a very windy place, like Wellington, and winter there is as cold as, if not colder, than Auckland. After my arrival in January, when I drove up to Eureka to fill a wrestling engagement, we passed through 200 miles of snow. Eureka is a lumbering district. The road passes through the biggest lumber mill in the world, so they told me. It extends right along the road frontage for about a mile and a half, with the mill office at one end.

This road lies through Redwood country - the world's biggest trees, so called. They used to tell me about these trees and I used to say "Well, they'll have to be pretty big to beat our Kauris."
When we came to them, I said "Do you call these trees big?" That shook them and they said, "There's some bigger ones further on." However, I told them some stories about our Kauris that maybe shook their confidence in the Redwoods. As a matter of fact, they are not as majestic as the Kauris. They don't have the great massive trunk or branch spread of the Kauri, but are just straight-stemmed trees with disproportionately small branches.

In all I had 80 contests - winning 62, drawing 10 and losing 8. Being the only New Zealander in the country, I found I had no difficulty in obtaining matches, and my style seemed to please the Yanks.
I met some of the leading United States wrestlers, including Jim Browning who beat me twice. Hans Steinke beat me and we also wrestled a draw. Hank Kaempfer beat me and I later reversed the decision. I took two decisions off old New Zealand favourite Stanly Pinto.

THE BIRTH OF THE OCTOPUS CLAMP.

There is no doubt that my specialty hold, the "octopus clamp" brought me more fans and wins than any other hold I know. This hold did not come about by accident. I worked hard on it for some time before I used it in public.

In 1936, the year the year of my hectic matches against Jack Forsgren, I met Glen Wade - one of the cleverest, but not spectacular, wrestlers in the country that year---in a match at Oamaru. During the progress of the match he caught me with a double-barred toehold. In an effort to inflict torture on Wade, I applied the same hold on him and the referee eventually had to separate us. (I understand that a similar incident occurred at the Detton-Meehan match in Wellington in August 1938, and referee Alf Jenkins - that sawn-off piece of human activity - had some bother untangling their legs.)

On returning to my hotel in Oamaru I could not get off to sleep. Through my mind kept running the possibility of adding another hold to my collection. But, I reasoned with myself, what's the use of a hold that ties both men in a knot? Well, I replied to myself, what would happen if I didn't bar both legs, just used one barred toehold and then stood up with it? I had no means of trying it out until I arrived back in Auckland, and then I lost no time in putting my idea into action.

I woke my brother Val, and told him of an idea I had for a good hold. He consented to be the victim and, after a bit of manoeuvering, I managed to apply what has since became famous as the "octopus clamp".

At that time I had no idea of the real affect the hold would have - it was more or less a dream child. But when I stood up and applied the pressure Val's hollering left no doubt in my mind that I had found a hold that was worth developing. Val was a sick man for several days after allowing himself to be the first victim of the clamp. Brotherly love.

I persuaded another brother Trevor, to be the victim until I had achieved sufficient pace for applying it in public. We used to work out in strict privacy until I managed to get adept at it. Then came the time when I decided to risk the hold in public.

The first time the octopus clamp was used in New Zealand wrestling was in Hamilton, but for the life of me I cannot remember the name of my opponent. Here let me wander off the beaten path for a moment. I have often been asked to give the names of the men I wrestled in America and have been criticised for not supplying the list. Honestly, I cannot recall the names of half the men I met over there, but if faced with a list of names I would have no hesitation in giving a fairly complete list - and accurate results. But a wrestler, wrestling two and three nights a week, cannot be expected to remember all his opponents. I make this point here because when I tell you I have forgotten the name of the first official victim of the clamp I hope I have convinced you that a wrestler cannot remember all the things some people expect he should.

Back to the clamp. I managed to get my opponent tied up in the clamp and he quickly conceded a fall. The referee, perhaps gifted with second sight, did not get in my way as I went about releasing the hold. To release the hold is just as difficult as applying it, and unless the referee knows how to go about the method of release he is more of a hindrance than a help.

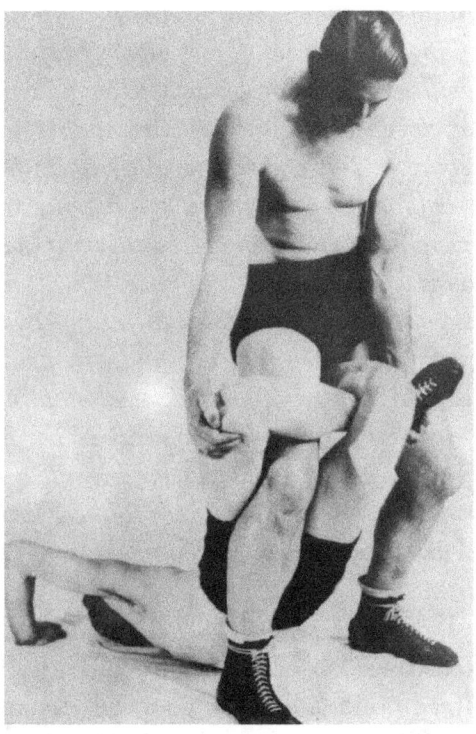

Lofty and his famous "Octopus Clamp"

My new hold did not get a great deal of publicity from Hamilton, although I was told later that the Hamilton correspondent of a national sporting paper, in describing it, wrote: *"It is similar to a boston-crab, only applied lower down and with the legs"*. Rather a complicated hold?

The next time the clamp was used was at Wellington where I met Paul Boesch, who introduced the standing drop-kick to New Zealand wrestling. I caught Boesch in the clamp at a time when I was facing the ropes, and when he conceded the fall I attempted to climb up the first rope to more easily release him. Referee Jenkins, thinking I was attempting to carry the hold a step further, pulled me back and penalised me a fall.

A portion of a press report of this match reads :

"To a mixed reception of boos and cheers, Lofty Blomfield, New Zealand heavyweight wrestling champion, was disqualified in his bout with Paul Boesch, in the Wellington Town Hall last night (May 25th 1936). In the seventh round Blomfield clapped on his octopus clamp when both men were near the ropes, Boesch conceded a submission fall almost immediately, and Blomfield was disqualified by the referee, Alf Jenkins for not making an effort to break the hold. At first Blomfield was inclined to dispute the decision, but he soon went forward and shook hands with Boesch, who was still lying on the mat nursing his badly twisted knee. When the hold was applied both men were in an almost inextricable tangle, and Boesch's right leg had to be freed by the referee after several ineffectual attempts. Mr. Jenkins said later that Blomfield had been disqualified for attempting a hold he could not break and for not making any effort to break it. For Blomfield it is said that the only way to break the hold was for Blomfield to walk forward: going sideways would only do more damage to the imprisoned leg. In this case, it was stated, the ropes prevented Blomfield from releasing Boesch in the only way he knew."

We had the dickens own job of getting Boesch out of the clamp, and as Boesch was already one fall to the good he was awarded the bout. Perhaps it is as well if I mention here that the practice of disqualifying a wrestler for an offence is against wrestling rules. It happened in Christchurch in 1938 when Detton was disqualified for the use of an alleged strangle but the Wrestling Union upset the decision. A guilty wrestler should be penalised one fall and if by reason of the infringement, the non-offending wrestler cannot continue - a second fall should be awarded. Although Alf Jenkins penalised me - he could be excused - I still felt confident that the clamp was my match-winning hold.

I went up to Gisborne where Tom Smale again disqualified me when I trapped Joe Woods in the clamp. Just as Alf Jenkins had imagined that I was not trying to release the hold, so did Tom Smale err. The fact of the matter is that I cannot release the hold unless given the room to work, and if I apply the clamp when facing up against the ropes I must climb them to get the pressure off my victim's legs and back.

With one win and two disqualifications for using the clamp I began to wonder if my hold was really worthwhile. Then came the best break of my career - two middle-aged gentlemen in Lower Hutt had an argument about the clamp. One was emphatic that it was impossible to escape from its clutches, the other was equally as confident that escape was easy. They decided to settle the argument by having a practical display. The strangest part of this strange affair was that the man who claimed it to be impossible to escape allowed his friend to put the clamp on him. Had he put the clamp on the one who said it was easy to escape, I would have understood it, but somehow or another, they reversed the logical order. A Wellington newspaper printed a report of the incident. At first I thought it was just a publicity gag, but couldn't think who was responsible. When I arrived in Wellington I learned that it was no publicity effort; that the incident had actually happened. To Senior-Sergeant Jack McHolm, former New Zealand amateur hammer-throwing champion, I was grateful for his action in letting the story reach the newspapers. As a result of this story the inescapable effects of the clamp received New Zealand-wide publicity. Here is what the paper had to say:

"A policeman at Lower Hutt was summoned urgently last night (June 12th 1936.) to unravel a human knot.

"Two well-known Lower Hutt residents, both keen followers of wrestling, experimented with Lofty Blomfield's much-discussed octopus clamp. Guided by diagrams and instructions, one man tried to put the hold on the other. He succeeded---and then, to his horror, he found he was unable to loosen it.

For fully ten minutes he manoeuvred gingerly, to his own discomfort and the intense suffering of the man on whom the hold was applied. It was useless; it was an octopus clamp and it remained as such. So must Lofty Blomfield have felt when he was disqualified in the Wellington Town Hall on May 25th. After he had so neatly applied the clamp to Paul Boesch, only to find that he could not disentangle it.

By this time both men were feeling the strain acutely. What could be done? One course suggested itself---the reliable policeman, the man to help one out of any trouble. A member of the family was quickly dispatched, and the policeman arrived to find two pain-stricken men mysteriously interlocked in an intricate mass of limbs.

The policeman was unhurried and calm, but effective. Within one minute he had the octopus clamp untied and the two exhausted would-be wrestlers lay back on the floor and panted their relief. The policeman unconcernedly returned to the police station. It was all in a days work after all."

It really is a great shame that Lofty did not get a great deal more of his story down on paper; I am sure there would have been many great tales to tell from the life of one of New Zealand's most popular wrestlers.

The following is an article I wrote on Lofty for 'Wrestling Review' around 1979:

In the late 1930s, New Zealand mat fans had hopes of seeing world champion Bronko Nagurski in a title match in New Zealand against their own champion Lofty Blomfield. Nagurski it is understood, had agreed to come to New Zealand for the largest guarantee ever offered a boxer or wrestler in the Southern Hemisphere. Plans had already been made to stage the match, which it was believed would attract more than 40,000 spectators.

The Dominion of New Zealand Wrestling Union, through Walter Miller, had been in negotiation with Nagurski and his backers - Toots Mondt, Lou Daro and Tony Stecher - and plans were on the verge of completion. However at the last minute, the mighty Nagurski had a change of plans and decided not to make the trip.

Perhaps Nagurski knew he was going to have a real battle whether he met Blomfield, Dean Detton or Ray Steele in New Zealand. Naturally, New Zealanders were hoping Blomfield would have been

Nagurski's opponent, but Lofty would have had to earn the right for this title match by beating the likes of Detton, Steele and Vincent Lopez.

Desperate for a title shot, Blomfield travelled to Canada - Vancouver, British Colombia, to be exact - and on March 17 1939 got a crack at Nagurski and the championship. The following report of Blomfield's title quest appeared in the March 18th edition of the Vancouver Sun:

"Lofty Blomfield, the gent from New Zealand, didn't exactly lift Bronko Nagurski's world crown before a packed house at the Auditorium last evening. But he did take a pretty hefty swipe at it, and his buddies from Down Under need, in no way, be ashamed of their champion.
For eight rounds last night, well on into the midnight hour, Nagurski and Blomfield put on one of the most entertaining matches seen here in a good many months.

When it was over they were no further ahead than when they started. It was a draw, with each man having taken a well-earned fall.
The two fellows, powerfully built and remarkably agile for their great size, sparred about displaying a variation of wrestling holds that kept the crowd well on their seats through the entire bout. It was straight squirming but the kind the customers liked.
Nagurski, the champion, had the edge through the early going and by the time the third round came around he had worked Blomfield into a spot. A couple of well-timed tackles, the kind Nagurski is reputed to dish out with great abandon on the professional gridirons of America, tossed the New Zealander for a loss.

In a groggy state, Blomfield got up off the mat only to walk into the powerful arms of Nagurski. The latter lifted his man with ease and slapped him to the matting several times before falling on him.
Stanley Myslasak, a squirmer of note in his own right, did the refereeing in the main bout last night and turned in a finished performance. He lost little time in beating out the three seconds in the third round as Nagurski pressed the New Zealander's shoulders.

With five more rounds to go, Blomfield quickly revived in his corner, came out with a greater determination and put the champion through many an anxious moment for the remainder of the bout.

During the fifth, sixth and seventh rounds, Blomfield harassed Mr. Nagurski very definitely with his famed octopus clamp. Numerous times he very nearly had the champion's legs tied up in tight little knots.

Turning on more heat in the eighth round, Blomfield went after Nagurski over every inch of the mat. He braved all the elbow jolts Nagurski threw in defence.

Finally, he succeeded in going behind the champion and slapped on the octopus clamp. Tying the champion's legs well and true, the New Zealander applied all the pressure he could and just before the bell sounded the end of the match, the champion yelled for mercy and conceded the tying fall.

It was a highly entertaining match to top off a first-class card presented by promoter Percy Hicks."

This was certainly the outstanding highlight of the great New Zealander's career. In later years, Blomfield chased Jim Londos for a title shot in New Zealand but it was impossible to attract Londos here. When Londos eventually did wrestle in New Zealand he was over 60 years of age.

Lofty Blomfield died in 1971 but he is not forgotten here and overseas. He met a host of American and Canadian wrestlers in New Zealand during his 20-year reign. Nearly thirty years after his death, Lofty was inducted into the New Zealand Sports Hall of Fame and (to date) is the only wrestler, amateur or professional, to be included.

Lofty (above) at home with some of his trophies. This family photograph was given to me by June Blomfield. (below) "Mein Host" at his hotel in Whangarei - this is the last photograph I took of Lofty.

Lofty Blomfield with Cecil B DeMille (second from left) - June Blomfield and Kay Bell on the set of the 1949 epic 'Samson and Delilah'. The movie starred Victor Mature in the starring role and Lofty's old friend Kay Bell was the Hollywood heart-throb's stunt double. This was during Lofty's final American tour and he retired permenantly from the wrestlng game the same year.

The chimps from Chipperfields Circus would visit the Whangarei Hotel every year to knock over the famous 'Penny Pile'. Lofty donated all of the pennies to the IHC charity.

Paul Boesch

Paul Boesch, the second world war's most decorated soldier-wrestler received six medals. The Silver Star and Cluster for gallantry in action, the Bronze Star for heroism, the Purple Heart and Cluster for wounds received in action, and the Combat Infantryman's Badge for exemplary conduct under fire.

This imposing list of awards caused the Commander of the 8th Infantry Division, Major General "Wild Bill" Weaver, to class his combat record as "distinguished" and further declared "His actions on the battlefield are superior in every instance. It is an honour to have him in my command."

In France, on his first day of combat, Paul won the Silver Star for moving forward and carrying one of his badly wounded men to safety.

In Luxembourg, Paul led a patrol into the Siegfried Line to gain information and although wounded by mortar fire, continued on the patrol until the mission was completed and the sought after information obtained.

In Germany, in an attack on the town of Hurtgen, Paul led the leading assault company across 700 yards of open ground that was swept by enemy machine-gun fire and plastered with artillery and mortar fire.

As a youngster Paul Boesch from Long Beach, New York, rescued over 500 people from the ocean. This amazing series of rescues started when Boesch was 14, on the beach in his home town, where the Atlantic Ocean manages to reach unbelievable peaks of fury at times. In the summer Paul loved being on beach patrol and helping rescuing people from the Atlantic.

A young Paul Boesch at the outset of his broadcasting career.

Wrestler Paul Boesch strikes a pose.

Paul came out to New Zealand on four occasions, three times as a professional wrestler, and once in 1984 as a guest commentator.

He first came here in 1936 and had some great battles with Earl McCready and Lofty Blomfield. In 1939 he came back having fallen in love with the country, and the many fans he had here.

After the war when wrestling got going again in New Zealand, Paul returned for the 1947 season to do battle with Kay Bell, Jim Wright, Tommy O'Toole, Jim Henry, Tom Rice, Otto Kuss and once again, Lofty Blomfield and Earl McCready.

Paul Boesch was a colourful character and his dropkicks and flying tackles were among the best to be seen here. When not wrestling, he was often on New Zealand radio. He had a beautiful speaking voice and listeners appreciated his between rounds commentaries.

Paul Boesch later in his broadcasting career (above left). The American legend was a wrestler, broadcaster, collector, historian, war hero, lifeguard and all-round good guy. Paul loved coming to New Zealand and we met up a number of times during his visits. The last time he visited was in 1984 when he was acting as guest commentator for the Rick Flair and Harley Race title matches. Above right is Paul's old school friend and former U.S. President, George Bush Snr. It was thanks to Paul that I received this signed photograph.

I got to know Paul very well as a pen-friend for countless years, and being a great collector of wrestling memorabilia we both had something in common. When he was asked to come out to New Zealand again in 1984 Paul jumped at the offer, and it was a great chance to show his second wife Valerie around the country he loved visiting so much as a wrestler. Paul came out here as a guest commentator for the Rick Flair-Harley Race N.W.A. World Title series. I recall meeting Paul and his family at Auckland Airport and it was a great pleasure to finally meet the man I had been corresponding with for many years.

Paul said his first mission was to hire a car and take his family to Rotorua, a place where he had had many wrestling contests in past years.

Paul Boesch and Kay Bell visit Earl McCready in 1983 - not too long before Earl died.

Paul Boesch and I in 1984, during his last visit to New Zealand.

The Forgotten Kiwis:
Unknown in their own country, but big stars around the world

In the 1930s some New Zealand wrestlers ventured to Australia as they were unable to get matches in their own country. Big Ernie Kingston, an Anton Koolman boy, did some service in the air force and ended up in England after the war. He became a huge success and wrestled all over Europe.

As an amateur boxer in New Zealand Ernie had been runner-up in the heavyweight division at the New Zealand Championships in 1938. He was also an outstanding rugby player and general all round sportsman. In England he was known as "Kiwi" Kingston. He perfected Earl McCready's pet hold the rocking chair splits, also known as the rolling scissors splits. The tall gangly Kiwi would roll his opponent around the ring half a dozen times before pinning their shoulders to the mat.

Ernie was one of the leading heavyweights in Europe. His matches with the legendary Bert Assirati are often talked about, and in the German tournaments he used to ride his horse up to the ring and dismount on the ring apron. Ernie spent his life around horses. He was in to show horses and was an outstanding horseman. Ernie told me his ambition was to drive a car across Europe, down through India, and across Australia, and come back to his birth place in Banks Penninsular, near Christchurch. However it was not to be, and he ended his days in Austria, dying some years back. Ernie was a special friend of ours and always a perfect gentleman.

Two rare photos of Kiwi Kingston: as New Zealand Jnr Heavyweight Champion (left) and later in a promotional photograph.

Other Kiwis who headed to Europe in 1949 were tall Tuakau farmer Ray Clarke, who was a good amateur and looked to have a good future in the professional ranks. He made a name for himself in Britain and met the legendary Bert Assirati on three occasions. Ray was also a musician, and always the life and soul of the party. He spent some years in Britain and around Europe and met the best they had to offer, including matches with Ray St Bernard, Kiwi Kingston, Ernest Baldwin, and Jack Pye. Before he returned to New Zealand Ray spent some time in Mexico, a hotbed of wrestling, where colorful masks were all the fashion. He moved on to Canada, where he was highly regarded.

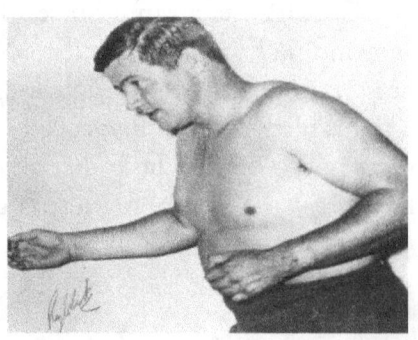

Ray Clarke

As I have said before it was nigh on impossible to break into the New Zealand circuit, even for a big six-footer like Ray. Ray came home in 1953 and tried his best for a couple of seasons. Walter Miller gave him a chance because he had fought all the leading wrestlers in Europe. However the style here was very much American style, and in 1954 Ray was having trouble getting bookings. He ended up joining the police force and for many years was the resident policeman on the Wanganella at Deep Cove in the deep south of the South Island.

Bob Russell, Ray Clarke and Russ Bishop in London at St Martins in the Fields (1949). All three were on their way to Manchester, where they were based. (photo courtesy of Bob Russell, living in Te Puke, New Zealand at the time of writing).

A couple of smaller boys left Auckland in 1949 with Ray Clarke. They were Bob Russell, a Maori boy from near Te Puke, and Russ Bishop, a middleweight from Auckland. Bishop, a tow-headed, hairy-chested amateur caused a sensation in Britain, and was claimed by the wrestling press as the "find" of the year. The British press had the following to say about Russ: "With superb physique and a dazzling style, the former bushman has attracted attention by the smooth collection of holds which he uses. To Bishop goes credit for the New Zealand "crab-hold" and the "frog scissors", both brand new to wrestlers and patrons, and he has mastered these two holds to perfection."

Bob Russell found the path to the top difficult to traverse, particularly for the lighter-weighted wrestlers. Finding English promoters rather disinterested in Bob Russell from New Zealand, the dark, pleasant looking Kiwi adopted an alias and became Prince Banu. He soon made the grade with his new name and was in demand all over Europe.

These boys worked the British and European circuits for some years, and as the smaller boys were in favour in Europe, they did very well and got heaps of bookings. On their way home they spent some time in Mexico, where they again proved the smaller boys could be great drawcards.

In New Zealand we were brought up on American heavyweights, but for sheer skill and all-action wrestling the smaller boys were amazing. During the early fifties the American style was not in favour in Europe. They preferred stylish, more skillful wrestling, with lots of holds and counter holds.

Bob Russell/Prince Banu
(photo courtesy of Bob Russell.)

Russ Bishop

Back in the very early 1930s a young Wanganui, and later Auckland policeman, by the name of Kingsley Elliott, was slowly climbing up the world wrestling ladder.

Wrestling was a very popular sport among members of the police force throughout New Zealand, and in 1931 many policemen were looking forward to wrestling in the amateur contests before the main professional bout. Wellington had a particularly good wrestler in Constable George Deacon, who had many successful contests.

King Elliott, the young Aucklander, went back to the United States with Tom Alley in 1930, and had some professional bouts with several wins. They went by ship, which was the way you travelled in the 1930s.

Upon arriving in Victoria, Canada on December 30 1930 he wasted little time in looking up master coach Virgil Hamlin in Portland, Oregon where, for two months, he went through a strict course of training. Leaving there he went to Seattle, where he won two matches, and then moved on to grapple in Cincinnati, Detroit, Louisville, Indianapolis, St Louis, Kansas City, and Dallas, Texas.

The young Aucklander won nearly all his bouts, and was regarded as a first-class grappler. His early weight of about 190lbs meant he could move freely about the ring, unlike the super dreadnoughts who came out here and were not so agile.

King came back to compete in his homeland in 1931, where each winter a selected team of American's would come and display their talents to "Kiwi" wrestling fans. King won some matches in New Zealand in 1931 beating Rocky Marshall in New Plymouth, Jack Higgins. He twice beat the flying Finn Alex Lundyn.

He cut his season here short and headed back to the United States, where he said he wanted to toughen up before meeting the top class talent that was brought to New Zealand.

King Elliott came here in 1931, 1932, 1935, 1936 and 1946, and in between spent much time in Australian rings, where he was a huge favourite. The following piece is from the Wellington Programme headed: "King Elliott is Good. Has taken Sydney by Storm."

"Next to Al Karasick, the most popular wrestler to visit Australia this year

has been the young King Elliott, the "Hurricane Tackler," who has packed out wherever he has appeared. Elliott is a vastly different matman from when he was last here. He is now a highly polished and spectacular wrestler whom the Sydney papers describe as a "marvellous grappler." Elliott is worth seeing. He is a New Zealander who has made good in U.S.A. and taken Sydney by storm. He is the goods is this young King Elliott.

Kingsley 'King' Elliott

Russian Lion Tom Lurich has had a number of close shaves during the present season at Leichhardt, but he got the shock of his life a fortnight ago, when young King Elliott held him to a draw. Elliott took the initial fall in the third round, and it was not until the final session that the Russian squared accounts."

In 1936 in a match in Invercargill the Southland paper had the following heading: "Octopus Clamp Squashes Elliott."

"Razzling" fans were treated to some real highlights of the mat game when Lofty Blomfield and King Elliott clashed for the New Zealand Heavyweight title. Elliott looked to have a mortgage on the title when the bout had gone half the journey. He was then well ahead on points with one fall up his sleeve, when Lofty came to light with his renowned octopus clamp. That was the end of Elliott for the evening."

King Elliott settled in the United States and after his spell here in 1946 we never saw him again. I have no idea what became of him. Like Pat O'Connor, another good Kiwi wrestler, he ended his days there.

New Zealand wrestler visits his homeland

New Zealand wrestler Johnny Lakey made a visit to his homeland in 2000 during the Christmas break, to visit his relatives and to show some of his American friends the great tourist sights of New Zealand.

John left New Zealand at the end of 1937, after having a few amateur bouts in Wellington, and some training with Anton Koolman, and made his mark as a professional wrestler in the U.S.A. He first headed for Australia and got a job on the 'S.S. Katoomba', which was trading around the Australian coast. He later worked on the 'Queen Mary' and the 'Queen Elizabeth', and his jobs included everything from "submarine watch" to working in the engine room.

During the late 1930s and early 1940s John got some work at the famous Leichhardt Stadium in Sydney, where all the leading boxers and wrestlers were seen.

When he hit the United States in 1946 he soon got work around the Chicago area for promoter Fred Kohler. Fred put on great matches each week at Chicago's famous Marigold Arena. Overnight New Zealander Johnny Lakey became Jack Carter of Australia. He travelled as Jack Carter all over the United States as a professional wrestler from 1946 to 1958. The promoters decided to change his name to Jack Carter and make him an Australian, as most Americans knew Australia.

Jack was known as a travelling wrestler, he stayed a few weeks and then moved to another territory, and in this way he never outstayed his welcome. Some wrestlers didn't like travelling and stayed in the same territory all their wrestling lives. In time the fans became sick of them and demanded new faces.

Born in Newmarket in Auckland, Jack was amazed at the changes when he came back on several occasions to visit his sister. Not surprisingly, being billed as an Australian wrestler, very few people ever knew he was from New Zealand. He was very well thought of in the United States as a leading tag-team wrestler and some of his partners were Ken Kenneth, Pat O'Connor and Jack O'Reilly. O'Reilly was another Kiwi-born wrestler who did well in the United States but was unknown in his own country. Jack was a protégé of the famous Anton Koolman in Wellington and as an amateur he was "Snow" Bartlett. When he turned professional he was "Irish" Jack O'Reilly of Australia. I saw Jack wrestle once in England when he was touring Europe.

Jack Carter met some of the top wrestlers in his heyday including Pete Bartu, The Mighty Atlas, Yukon Eric, The Elephant Boy, George Drake, Billy Darnell, Angelo Poffo, Vern Gagne, Buddy Rogers, "Gorgeous" George, and Dave Levin. He was billed to meet World Champion Lou Thesz, the Hungarian great, when he had the misfortune to break his leg, which necessitated a long layoff from the mat game.

Two of Jack Carter's famous opponents - Gorgeous George (above) and Nature Boy Rogers (below).

Hans Schnabel (right) who wrestled in a tag-team with Jack Carter in the 1940s.

When Jack retired from wrestling in 1958 he took over a gas station and many of his old opponents called in for a chat. He maintained his interest in doing up old cars and had a couple of speedboats in Florida, where he loved to get out on the water.

Jack Carter during a visit in 1990, seen here studying one of my many scrapbooks. Jack loved looking though my collection as there was pleanty of stuff on him and the famous wrestlers he met in the ring.

Jack met up with boxing great Jack Dempsey on several occasions when Jack was refereeing wrestling contests, and he was most impressed with Dempsey. He also knew Primo Carnera, another heavyweight boxing champion, and they appeared on the same programme on many occasions. Some of his favorites were Dean Detton, Gene Stanlee, Dick the Bruiser, and Jack Claybourne. He had a lot of time for Jack Claybourne (who was a smaller heavyweight like himself) and was in big demand around Texas, Mississippi and Chicago. He was frequently used by Fred Kohler and Joe Malcewicz, both leading wrestling promoters of the day.

Jack Carter at our home around 2000 - his last trip to his home country. My wife Shirley and I always loved having Jack over for a visit.

It was great for me to catch up with one of the sport's great characters, especially as he was born in New Zealand. He had seen my articles in various American wrestling publications and tracked me down on one of his visits. After that he made sure he called on me every time he came home.

"Blind Peter"
and
Gordon Hutter

Peter Morelatos or "Blind Peter" as he was known to Radio 1YA wrestling fans in the 1930s, was born in Greece, and came to New Zealand as a young man in 1902. He was blinded in an accident in 1925 after spending years as a fisherman in various parts of New Zealand.

The famous partnership of Gordon Hutter and Peter Morelatos extended well beyond the wrestling ringside. When "Blind Peter" got married, Gordon was his best man, and they remained lifelong friends.

Gordon Hutter (above left) with "Blind Peter" Morelatos in their familiar ringside location.

After the partnership with Gordon Hutter ended, Peter teamed up with Bill Mudgeway. Bill did wrestling commentary with Peter as well as professional boxing from Auckland Town Hall and the YMCA. He also did the speedway from Western Springs for 45 years. Later in life Mudgeway became the "Eye in the Sky" for radio I (starting in 1981) and for 13 years he reported every 15 minutes during the morning and evening rush-hour traffic. Bill estimated that he spent 13,000 hours in a small Cessna patroling the skies above Auckland.

Bill Mudgeway (above left) with 'Blind' Peter Morelatos

www.ingramcontent.com/pod-product-compliance
Lightning Source LLC
LaVergne TN
LVHW051559070426
835507LV00021B/2672